CREATOR · GOD · SUSTAINER · PROTECTOR

FOUR STEPS TO PURE IMAN

Explanations of a Painting

by His Holiness
M. R. Bawa Muhaiyaddeen

THE FELLOWSHIP PRESS
Philadelphia, PA

Library of Congress Cataloging in Publication Data

Muhaiyaddeen, M. R. Bawa.
   Four steps to pure iman.

   Includes index.
   1. Sufism.   I. Title.
BP189.2.M79   1981   297'.4   81-1429
                                          AACR2

Copyright © 1979 by the Bawa Muhaiyaddeen Fellowship
Philadelphia, Pennsylvania

All rights reserved. No portion of this book
may be reproduced in any manner without
written permission from the publisher.

Printed in the United States of America
First Printing 1979
Second Printing 1981

His Holiness M. R. Bawa Muhaiyaddeen

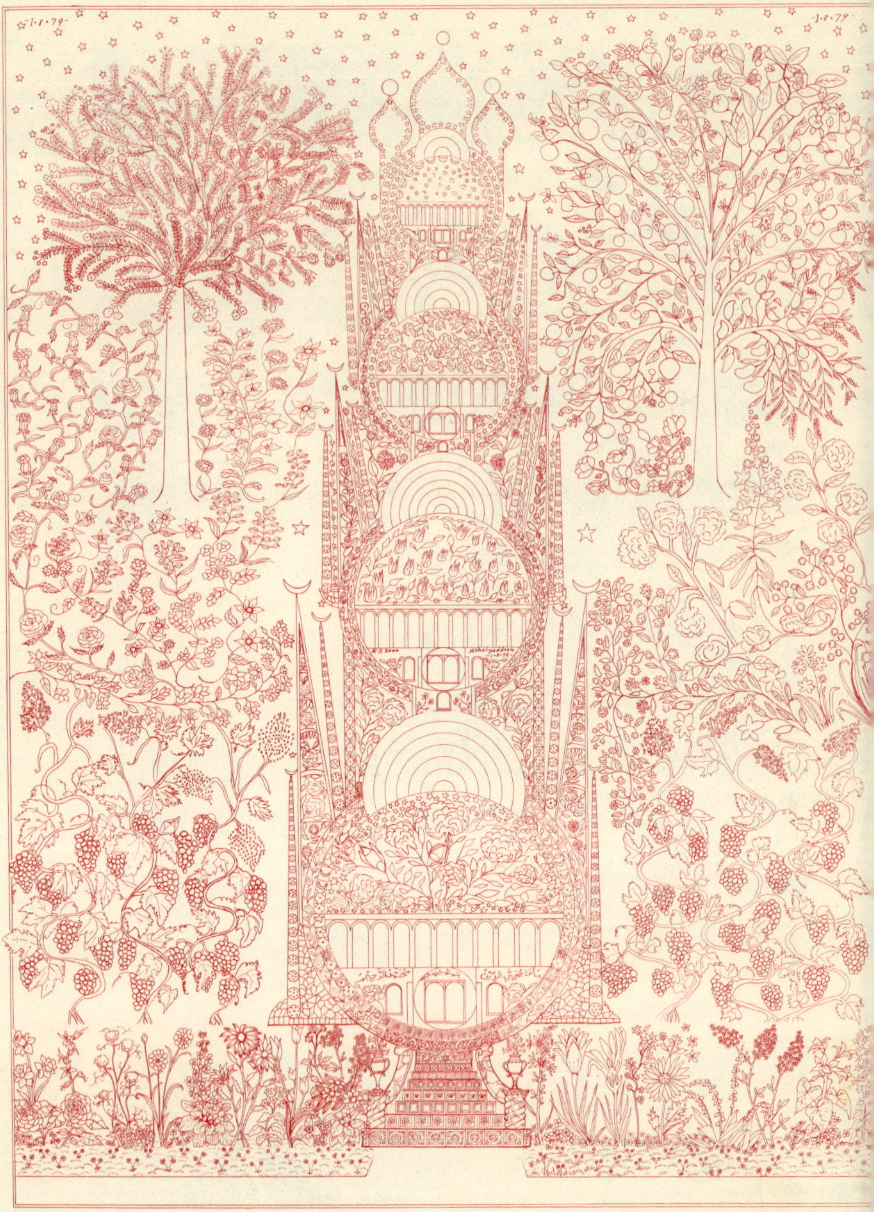

Contents

THE FOUR RELIGIONS	1
TRUE PRAYER	17
THE MYSTICAL MIRROR	33
GLOSSARY	47
INDEX	67

The Four Religions

B*ismillāhirahmāniraheem:* In the name of God, the Most Merciful, Most Compassionate.

Loving children, jeweled lights of my eyes, I have painted a picture which is an illustration of God's house, of the place in which to pray, of the mosque for prayer, and of the way to prayer. This painting has many meanings. You have been asking about it, and therefore, I am giving you this small explanation.

God has no form. He has no equal. He does not possess the six evils of lust, hatred, miserliness, greed, bigotry, and envy. He is the One who existed in the time of darkness before the beginningless beginning. He is the One who has no birth and no death. He is the One who has not been created and will never be destroyed. He is the One who rules alone. He is the One who has created all creations, the One who protects them, who nourishes and watches over them. He is the Compassionate One. For His might and for His duty there is no comparison, and there is no praise which is sufficient. He does His duty formlessly. He is incomparable and unequaled. Thus He shows His compassion, and thus He does His duty. One who is like this is called God. That God has made all life to arise, and He loves all lives and watches over them.

Within the heart of each creation, there is a point which is automatically aware of God. Even if we forget God, there is a force within the body which makes us remember. That point of God comes at times of forgetfulness. It is intermingled within the tissues of the body itself. Even one who says, "There is no God," is reminded of Him by that minute point within the flesh. It is an awareness that exists when a danger or an accident approaches. That point within the flesh trembles and tells us to believe in Him. That point is made of light, and God has placed it within the body.

God has placed that piece of flesh closer to us than our own lives, and God is within it, even smaller than that minute point. Truth, light, God, and His power exist there in perfect equality. That place gives warning from within the body; it reminds us of God and gives us explanations of the path on which we walk. At one time, a warning might come. At another time, it might make us realize a fault we have committed. At still another time, it protects us from danger. Like that, there is this power which protects human beings, and that power is God. He exists as light within wisdom, as the clarity within wisdom and perfection, as the light within the light of the eyes, as taste and speech within the tongue, as sweet speech, as the beauty of the face, as the sweet sound within the ears, as the sweetness within the nose, as a wafting fragrance, a very fragrant fragrance within the nose, as that piece of flesh within the heart, as the power of grace, as the resplendent *Noor* [the resplendence of Allah], as the explanation.

This awareness exists in each section. It exists in the hands. It is the hand of *Īmān* [absolute faith, certitude, and determination] and *Rahmat* [unfathomable grace], the hand which gives and gives without ever diminishing, the hand which exists as absolute plenitude. In the legs, this awareness exists in two ways, as two legs which walk with two different intentions. One leg is in this world, and the other leg is in the next world. With those two legs, we are shown how to hold up the leg of the physical world and walk on the leg of the next world. Allah is the One who explains this from within mankind. He gives that explanation of wisdom.

When Allah was creating Adam, He formed and placed the light known as *Noor* on the forehead of Adam. That spot on the forehead is the *Kursī*, the eye of *Gnānam* [Divine Luminous Wisdom]. That is the complete resplendence which Allah has revealed. That is the eye which can directly see Allah. *Gnānam* is the tongue of *Imān* which can directly speak to Allah. That is the face of beauty and the resplendence of perfection. That is the eye of *Gnānam*, which is known as the *Noor*, and was placed on the forehead of man at the time of creation. It has been placed within everyone, and it looks at everything from within. God has created human beings in this state. He has made them complete, and He has established that beauty.

Within man there is darkness and light, wisdom and ignorance, truth and lies, human beings and animals, wisdom and false wisdom, life and true life, a true existence and a false existence, a true body and a false body, true meditation and true prayer, false meditation and false prayer, true miracles and false miracles, true qualities and false qualities, the compassionate qualities of God's praise and the qualities of the deceptive praise of the world. Man is subject to so many different kinds of actions. He is subject to truth and falsehood. As long as he does not understand the difference between truth and falsehood, all his meditations and prayers will exist as falsehood. It is from such meditations that the many religions have developed.

Allah created one Adam. The prophets that came to teach God's truth were many, and they taught only about the One God and His commandments. But people looked at the levels of the prophets' wisdom, began to worship the separations, and created religious differences because of these separations. There were devotional differences and differences in prayers. The one race was divided into many races, the One God was made into many gods, the one truth was forgotten and divided into many falsehoods, and all this they believed to be devotion. The truth of the One God and one family was changed, and many tens of millions of religions, many tens of millions of races, many tens of millions of scriptures, tens of millions of kinds of worship, tens of millions of kinds of prayer, tens of millions of kinds of miracles were started. Those miracles, those yogas, those wisdoms, those mantras, those magics, those tricks, those tens of millions of idols, those prayers— all those separations came to be and were divided into the four religions of *Zaboor, Jabrāt, Injeel,* and *Furqān.*

The first religion is *Zaboor*, or Hinduism. The second is *Hanal* or *Jabrāt*, the worship of fire. The third is *Injeel*, or Christianity, the religion of those who worship many spirits. The fourth is the religion of *Furqān*, or Islam, the religion of those who worship Light. The one religion was divided into four, and the four were also divided into so many divisions. Each religion was divided and divided and divided. Within Hinduism are tens and tens of millions of sects. Even now, so many different forms of prayers exist in the Hindu religion and in the religion of Fire Worship. In the religion of Christianity, look at how many different kinds of Bibles there are, how many different kinds of prayers and kinds of worship. And within Islam, or *Furqān*, so many divisive actions have taken place. But even though Islam has these many divisions, at least they do have the certitude that there is only one God.

There are many wondrous places which people call places of worship. They call them churches, temples, mosques, and many other things. For the four religions, four different places of worship have been built. Amongst these places of worship, those who want to do the easy prayer stand in the first level, the first mosque. Because they cannot see the One God who has no form, they worship everything. In the first mosque, each man thinks about God, prays to Him, and tries to see Him. But the demons, the ghosts, the satans, the scorpions, the crabs, the idols, the darknesses, the seas, the oceans, the sun, the moon, the stars, the mountains, the flowers, the trees, the jinns, the fairies, the angels, the heavenly beings, and many tens of millions of things are there. They live in that place. They also live within the body in the form of dark shadows. There is a place like that within each human being. On the outside, God has created them as forms. There they exist as scenes, as formed things.

That is the first religion of *Zaboor*. Those things all live in that church. Everything is worshiped in that church. Why? Because everyone takes his own aspect with him and prays in his own way to these four hundred trillion, ten thousand things with four hundred trillion, ten thousand spiritual prayers. That is the worship of demons, the worship of animals, the worship of dogs, the worship of cats, the worship of rats, the worship of satans, the worship of darkness, the worship of the sun, the worship of the moon, the worship of the stars, the worship of demonic forces, the worship of ghosts. They are all worshiped there. Any kind of worship can be performed there. Their mantras, their songs, their meditations, their yogas, their miracles—all are performed to snakes, scorpions, oceans, lands, to illusion, darkness, fascination, lust and passion, to demons which drink blood, ghosts, and tens of millions of things like them. That is what is worshiped there. They stand in that worship with four hundred trillion, ten thousand kinds of separations, and they make idols which are suitable to each aspect. No matter what god anyone needs, he first sees the form within himself, then he creates that form on the outside and worships it. That method is very easy for everyone. Those who are in that state and go to that temple are like that. That is *sharī'at* [the first step of spiritual ascendance].

The next mosque is the worship of fire, the *Hanal* religion. They place fire gods, sun gods, moon gods, and many tens of millions of gods like that in their temple and worship them.

Third is the *Injeel* religion, the religion of Christianity. In the religion of Christianity, they started out with one Bible but divided it into many and created so many separations. There are many spirits and many miracles in Christianity. They attribute miracles to the spirits. They believe in such things, worship them, and sing songs to them. Within the churches, they also use wine and intoxicants. They worship like this in the third mosque.

The next level is the mosque of Islam, or *Furqān*. But really, all these four mosques are mosques of *sharī'at*. If you look at all four religions, you can tell that they are all *sharī'at*. The mosque of Islam is *sharī'at*. They say that there is only one God, but they each search for miracles and powers when they go to pray. They complain about the things they lack. They pray for wives, children, livestock, property, and material possessions. They worship God by asking for these things. This is the *sharī'at* level of Islam. Some pray five times, others pray three times, others pray seven times, but what do they ask for? They ask for the things that they want in this world. They want to perform miracles, they want a wife, they want money, they want a house, they want property, they want material possessions, they want a good life, they want titles, they want honors, they want their wives to be healthy, they want to be healthy, they want to take vengeance on others, they want to lie about others, and they want to steal. They pray like that in *sharī'at*. That is the state in which they live, and that is what they search for in their worship.

They call this prayer, worship, devotion, religion, the Qur'an, the Bible, the *purānas*, and many other names. Each section is divided into so many other sections. This is the state which now exists as worship in the world. This is what we have seen. The destruction caused by fire, the destruction caused by earthquakes, the destruction caused by rain, the destruction caused by gales, the destruction caused by famine, the destruction caused by polluted and poisonous air—all kinds of destruction are very widespread. Famine, hunger, poverty, and all these difficulties and accidents have come about because of the way in which people worship. People bring these things upon themselves. The world is destroying itself through these accidents.

In this state, in *sharī'at*, there are these four different kinds of mosques. They worship according to caste, they worship the elements, they worship idols, they worship money, they worship blood-ties, they worship material possessions, they worship the earth, they worship miracles, they worship the land, they worship many tens of millions of gods, they worship many idols, and they worship many tens of millions of kinds of false wisdom which they call *gnānam*. But really, they worship lack of wisdom, *agnānam*, or ignorance. They worship monkeys, they worship donkeys, they worship dogs, they worship cats, and many things like them. They have countless gods and countless miracles. They worship miracles performed by ghosts, miracles performed by blood-sucking demons, the miracles of satan, and gods which can be seen by their eyes. They make forms which are acceptable to their minds, and they worship them.

That kind of worship is performed in the mosques of *sharī'at*. What each one brings with him is his god. They create countless gods, and pray to them in any way they want. They pray to have the ability to perform miracles. They subjugate jinns, they subjugate demons, they subjugate ghosts, they subjugate satan, and they subjugate animals. They subjugate so many things and perform miracles through that subjugation. The miracles correspond to the qualities of what they control. They see the miracles, they praise the miracles, and they enjoy them. This is what exists in the *sharī'at* level of the mosques of the four religions. It is those miracles which they praise and which fascinate them. They praise them, they see them, and they enjoy them. In the world, that is what the majority of people do. That is what they like. That is what many desire. But that is not prayer! It is only *sharī'at*.

Prayer does exist in all four religions; it has been made into four kinds of worship. The first is the aspect of prayer in the *Zaboor* religion, or the Hindu religion. Let us look at the meditation and prayer that they perform in this mosque. In this mosque, those who come to pray and those who come to this state of meditation like many millions of miracles. That is why they pray. About 99%, or 9,999,990 out of ten million, pray in this house of *sharī'at*. They make tens of millions of idols, according to what is in the mind of each. They become fascinated and involved with miracles. They become involved with mantras and yoga. They worship form on the outside and shadowy formlessness on the inside. They have both these sections. Inside, they have the form of darkness, and outside, they have the created form. They worship this, they do *pūjās* [ritual devotions] and prayers. In ten million, there might be ten people who can go beyond this state. Out of ten million, 9,999,990 people worship in that first mosque of *sharī'at* and call it meditation. That is their meditation or prayer, their religious worship.

There are the four levels of *sharī'at*, *tarīqat*, *haqīqat*, and *ma'rifat*. They are within you, and this painting shows these levels of prayer.

Where do these prayers lead? If you come to the state of true meditation and you look at this state of *sharī'at*, the miracles and the energies, the yogas, and the arts which they talk about, all have forms. They take form on the inside, then the forms are brought to the outside and people begin to worship them. They say that it is a *sakti*, or an energy, and an ability which comes from God. They say it is a demonic energy, an elemental energy, a magic energy, the energy of the sun, the energy of the moon, the energy of fire, the energy of water, or the energy of illusion. They make gods like that, and they ask for boons and miracles. That is their meditation. They stay in caves and sit there under trees and bushes. They sit there and meditate like this. They worship and then they go away. People make them swamis or saints; they give them such titles. Very many people are like that. Maybe ten out of ten million are not in that state. If you leave that and go beyond, next there is the *Hanal* religion and *tarīqat*.

Taripādu [Tamil] or *tarīqat* [Arabic] means to make your *Īmān* firm, to make firm the absolute belief in God. At the second level of *tarīqat*, your *Īmān* should be made firm. But this level is also the state of Fire Worship. Here the fire of hunger, the fire in air, the fire in water, and the fire in old age is what fascinates. In that fascinating torpor, you are hungry, you run here and you run there, you search, and you meditate. The search for the food of determination, for the prayer of certitude, for determined faith, for the certitude that God has created everything and that He will provide the food is all forgotten. *Īmān* is forgotten. Many have separated into that state. At this level, there are not even five out of ten million who escape from the vapors and spirits. At the level of *tarīqat*, only five out of ten million establish *Īmān*, and maybe not even that many.

Next, the third prayer is the level of *haqīqat*, or Christianity. When one comes to the place of *haqīqat*, the *Īmān*, the certitude and the determination to merge with God, should exist. The *Īmān* that God and we must be one, that we must live as one and merge as one, should exist at that level. When you go to the station of *haqīqat*, that *Īmān* and that merging should be happening. But when you look around, all you see is miracles, demons, and spirits. There are four hundred trillion, ten thousand spirits which are within the body. The spirits within the body and the energies which travel outside the body, the demonic spirits, spirits of earth, air, fire, and water, and all the things which are intermingled with the *rūhānī* [the elemental spirit] are still present at this level. In that place they say, "Spirit, spirit, pure spirit!" They call out to the spirits and worship them at this third station. But they do not know which spirit, they do not know which god, they do not know which idol, they do not know which lord they are calling to. They say, "Spirit, spirit!" They say, "God, God!" and they pray. But they do not know which god they are worshiping, they do not know what God is like, they do not know who God is, and they do not worship in accordance with that awareness. They come to this third level, they become fascinated, and they change. There are not even two people out of ten million who escape from that! There are not even two people out of ten million who truly perform worship in that state of *haqīqat*.

The next level is Islam, or *ma'rifat*. These are the four levels of *sharī'at, tarīqat, haqīqat,* and *ma'rifat*. When you go from the level of *sharī'at* to the level of *ma'rifat*, you go without day or night, without energies or miracles, without pride or praise, without titles or honors. You believe that there is only one God, and you believe in the treasure which is the one way to merge with God. That is the soul. That is the truth. And that is the *Īmān* and certitude that only purity can merge with God. Nothing else will merge with God. Nothing else will mingle with God.

God is the pure One. He has no form, He has no shape, He has no color, He has no hue, He has no race, He has no religion, He has no differences, He has no insanity, He has no fascination, He has no equal, He has no relations, He has no children, He has no possessions, He has no pleasure, He has no sadness, and He has no happiness. He is the pure One, the undiminishing One, the One who wants nothing. He is the endless One, the indestructible One. He is the One who exists forever. He is God, *Allāhu*, the One who is that one resonance. He is the One who gives the explanation and the One who is alone. God is purity, He is perfection, and He is plenitude. At the fourth level, prayer, meditation, and worship are for purity to merge with purity and for plenitude to merge with plenitude.

Like that, whatever God has within Him is what will merge with Him and mingle with Him. What does not exist within God will not merge with God. The power which is God is one power. It is a power which He has decreed—the power of wisdom, the power of *Īmān*, the real power, the power of light. It is these rays of light which can merge with God, and that is the state of *vanakkam, 'ibādat, Zikr,* and *Fikr* [prayer, worship, remembrance, and contemplation]. That is *ma'rifat*. And for that prayer there is no race, no religion, or difference. There are no colors, hues, or religions. There is only one family and one God. It is that one power which is God. There is no equal and no comparison to Him. He is the unfathomable ruler of grace and the One who is limitless love. He protects everything. That one truth, that one *qalb* [innermost heart], and that one certitude in which the plenitude merges with the plenitude is called *ma'rifat*.

In the state of *ma'rifat*, there is no night and no day. There is no night and no day. There is no end. And for one who has no day and no night, there is no age, and he has no needs. He is always young, and that is why his prayer has no day and no night. That is *ma'rifat*, the state which has no race or differences, no hunger, no old age, no disease, no death, no 'you', no 'I', and no scriptures. Prayer without any of these things is the prayer of purity, the perfect prayer. That is *ma'rifat*, where one intermingles with the One and the truth within God. To merge with that plenitude is prayer. To worship the treasure within God is *ma'rifat*. That is when perfection merges with perfection.

These are the four steps to prayer and the meaning of this picture. The religions have all divided from each other. They are all separate. People worship their own qualities as gods, and they make them into idols. Within the divisions, there are many tens of millions of gods, many tens of millions of miracles, many tens of millions of heavenly beings, four hundred trillion, ten thousand gods and idols and miracles which exist as the energy of the earth, the energy of the demons, the energy of the elements, the energies and the miracles of the creations of God. But these things will all change. They will all be destroyed, and those who pray to them will also be destroyed. They appear in certain times, and when the times change, they disappear just like a crop which grows in one season and is cut down in another. Those are the prayers and miracles which can be destroyed. If you grow those crops of destruction within, eventually they will be destroyed and their miracles will also be destroyed.

There is a pearl within an oyster. If the pearl matures, then the oyster can no longer exist. It is destroyed. Similarly, no matter how many miracles one can perform, there will come a time when they will kill him. The miracles themselves will kill the one performing them. Those energies which he tries to subjugate will in turn destroy him. But there is a God who transcends those energies. If He is reached, that is the pearl. That is liberation. That is the kingdom of God. Only the state of existing as God within God has no destruction. There is no season for that, no time, no attachment, no equal, and no comparison. That alone is the harvest which has no season. That is the harvest which does not grow in the earth, the harvest which is indestructible and undiminishing. Such perfection is true prayer, and it must be seen with the eyes of purity and without the elements of destruction. Everything else is like weeds growing in the earth. The mantras, the *tantras* [tricks], the miracles—all of them grow in one season and in the next season they are destroyed. As each new crop comes up, the old crops are destroyed. As each new miracle comes up, the old miracles are destroyed. As they come up, they must be cut and harvested. A flower will bloom for a certain time, and later it will be destroyed. These energies, these miracles, all this praise, all these prayers, all these kinds of devotion, all these kinds of beliefs, all these yogas, all these arts—all of them will change and be destroyed.

Other than the power of the One God, everything else will be destroyed. That is what we must realize. In that state, only one thing will remain and only one thing will be prayer. Nothing else will be prayer. We have to realize that the religions are all crops which will be destroyed. Each thing that we see grow will later be destroyed, even though we may have praised it. Each animal, each donkey, each horse, no matter how well it is trained will be destroyed when its time comes. No matter how beautifully you sow a crop, it will begin to rot as soon as it matures. Grass that grows soon dries. No matter what you see in each season, all are crops which are destructible.

There are four seasons. There are four kinds of air. In one kind of air certain crops appear, and they disappear in the next kind of air. One season they appear and the next season they are destroyed. Look at all the crops. They are all destructible! All these miracles and these energies are destructible. All these devotions, these creations, these blood-ties, these beliefs, these material possessions, these relationships, these races, these religions, and these differences exist in this state.

Therefore, whoever grows these crops will exist in the hell of this earth world. Whoever grows these diminishing crops, whoever prays the prayers of these diminishing crops, whoever does the meditation of these diminishing crops, whoever performs the yoga or the arts or the sciences or the miracles, whoever has these things will never leave hell. He will be intermingled with the earth from which these things appeared. Wherever the earth is, he will be.

This is not worship. This is not prayer or meditation or worship. Prayer is to overcome all the elements and the demons and the energies within oneself. It is very difficult, and not everyone will be able to do this. Those who join with these divided sections will not accomplish this. But one who makes his certitude strong, one who goes beyond the four steps to intermingle with God is called *Insān Kāmil*, or perfected man. It is an *Insān Kāmil* who is a man of wisdom. In this state the four religions must be transcended, the four kinds of worship must be transcended, and man must merge with God. That is prayer. That is worship [*toluhay*]. That is devotion ['*ibādat*]. If you look at this state, you will see that this transcends the four religions and merges with God. To speak with God and to intermingle with Him is the state of *sūfīyat*. To merge with Him, to stand beyond all those things is *sūfīyat*. This is the fifth level, the state of *Īmān*, of absolute faith, certitude, and determination. This is the state of embracing God. This is the state of intermingling with and speaking to God.

The mosques in these pictures reveal the four steps [*sharī'at, tarīqat, haqīqat,* and *ma'rifat*]. Together these are the houses of God, the house of prayer. We have to build this within. We have to climb up and pray, transcending and going beyond all these differences. We have to climb each step and go within. We have to transcend each step and reach the purity which reaches God.

This example has been shown for the mind. There is a great deal more to be explained about it; I have only given a brief explanation. But if you can understand this much, at least try to form this within your heart. This is how we must worship, progressing step by step and transcending each step. We have to intermingle with what must be intermingled with and merge with God who is beyond *sūfīyat*. I have shown you this so that you may become one with Him and come to that state of speaking with Him.

This is not a simple picture. It has very many deep meanings which must be realized. You must build them within your hearts, step by step. Even though only ten out of ten million transcend the first level of *sharī'at*, you must transcend that level. But the majority likes the state of *sharī'at*; they like worshiping cats and dogs. At the second level, only five out of ten million transcend it. The rest all remain there in the state of *tarīqat*. And only two transcend the third level; the rest all remain in *haqīqat*. And in *ma'rifat*, it is difficult for even one to reach what must be reached.

Therefore, this is how determinedly you must pray. It will be good if you have that certitude. That is why I have painted this picture. Prayer has to be done this way. The flower garden has to be like the one in the painting. In this flower garden, many fruits have to be taken from one tree. But no matter how many colors there are, it is the sweet taste that must come. Like the many fruits on these trees, prayer exists in one place. On the tree known as God's grace, there are many fruits which must be plucked and eaten. On one tree, there are many flowers which we must see. In the one state of *Gnānam* [Divine Luminous Wisdom], we must see all the people in all the universes as one people, as one family. In one place, we have to perceive one sweet taste. Like that, within us, all creation must be perceived as one taste. We must see all creation with one eye. Just as all the different fruits are on this one tree, everything must be received from God. All taste must be perceived in God. That is perfectly pure *Gnānam*.

The state of prayer is like this flower garden and like this tree. God's house is inside, inside the flower garden. You have to build this house in a good way and go up, step by step. Make it beautiful, open it, and see the path on which God is reached. That will be good. That is why I have given you this small explanation. There is a lot more. This is just the aspect of the states of prayer. The mosques of the religions are one way, but the mosques in which true prayer is performed, the mosques within, are like this.

Sharī'at, tarīqat, haqīqat, and *ma'rifat* have to exist inside. This is the prayer within. Outside are the prayers of the religions. This is what we must realize.

Children, you must try to progress. Establish your *Īmān* with certitude. Try to progress. Climb up. That will be good. Ameen.

True Prayer

B*ismillāhirahmānirāheem.*
Children, do you remember what I was telling you earlier? Now I am going to tell you more about the methods of prayer. Prayer is purity. Praying while knowing how to pray is true prayer. What is prayer like? In what state does it take place? How should we pray? Who prays? To whom do we pray? Who accepts prayer? Who is He? What is He? Whom are we worshiping? Who accepts our prayers? What is prayer? All this we must understand.

The basic point is that God has created the world. He has created the world of heaven, this world, and the world of the soul. Why did God create these? He created them as examples. With our eyes, we can see the creations in the world, but there are also creations that cannot be seen. Some creations we see through desire, others we see through our *rūh* [soul] and *rūhāni* [elemental spirit], some we see in our dreams, and some we cannot see at all. They exist in the earth, in the sky, in the hereafter, and in the world of the soul. We have to reflect on this a little.

Children, my precious children, only after we know how to pray does prayer take place. That is what is called worship. Prior to knowing this, we may think we are praying, but everything we do is only practicing. All our learning, all our reciting is just practice. As we progress, such practice might help to bring true prayer into our awareness, it might help bring prayer into our memory, it might bring prayer into wisdom, and it might bring prayer into *Īmān* [absolute faith, certitude, and determination].

God has said that prayer is first to have absolute certitude in God, then to accept God, to know Him after you accept Him, to pray to Him after you know Him, and to merge with Him after praying to Him. This happens in the same way that firewood is no longer firewood after it is put into the fire. After the firewood is consumed, only the fire remains. Like that, in prayer when your thoughts are consumed, when your intentions are consumed, when your desires, your attachments, your connections, and your blood-ties are all consumed and burned in prayer, then God alone will exist and nothing else. The 'I' will not be there. That is the *daulat* or the wealth of prayer, the wealth of true meditation. When this state is established, then we can know prayer, then we can know God, and we can understand what a human being is.

Allah has given an illustration. He has said, "I have 3,000 beautiful qualities of grace. I have given 1,000 to the angels and 1,000 to the prophets. I have given 300 to the *Zaboor* religion, the religion of Hinduism. I have given 300 to the *Jabrāt* religion, the religion of Fire Worship. I have given 300 to the *Injeel* religion, the religion of Christianity. And I have given 99 of My qualities to *Furqān*, the religion of Islam. The qualities I have given to *Furqān* are My actions, the performance of those actions, and My *wilāyats* [powers]. These three are combined together and given as the 99 qualities to *Furqān*. But I have kept one quality in My own hand. That quality entails judgment, acceptance, protection, and giving sustenance. I have distributed all My other powers. This is the one quality that I have kept in My hand alone."

This is what Allah has said and proven. These qualities have been given to the four religions and to the places in which they worship. These 3,000 qualities of grace, the 99 *wilāyats* or powers of Allah, His actions, His qualities, and His behavior—all these will be in the hand of one who is a true human being. If one reaches purity in his prayer, then these 3,000 qualities of grace will be within him. His 99 *wilāyats*, His actions and behavior will all exist within one who is *Insān Kāmil* [perfected man]. It has all been given to one who is a *gnāni* [a man of wisdom].

What is a wise man? What is one who knows true

prayer like? Allah has explained and revealed this through Prophet Muhammad (*Sal.*). At one time, the idol worshiping Abu Jahil [first cousin and enemy to Muhammad (*Sal.*)] commanded that Muhammad (*Sal.*) be killed. He tried to harm the Prophet (*Sal.*) in many ways. He tried to ambush him and tried to kill him in open battle, but he failed in all attempts. Then he thought, "In any path, no matter what we try to do to Muhammad or to his disciples, all my intentions go wrong. No matter which of our warriors we send before Muhammad, as soon as they see him, they bow to him. Everyone who goes to Muhammad bows to Muhammad. Everyone is submissive to Muhammad. Therefore," he concluded, "he must be a great magician or a sorcerer. That is how he controls everyone who goes before him." And Abu Jahil declared to everyone that Muhammad (*Sal.*) was a magician.

But Allah disproved this by saying, "Of the 1,000 gracious qualities I have given the prophets, one is this quality which makes everyone who confronts the Prophet bow to him. It is not sorcery. It is not magic."

The powers of Allah, His intentions, His thoughts, and His words will radiate from one who has those true qualities. No matter what opposition comes, no matter what kind of fighting comes, no matter what opposes him, no matter how much enmity exists toward him—as soon as his enemies see him, they will bow down, and their *Īmān* will be strengthened. The qualities with which they came will leave them, and they will take into themselves good qualities and become good people. They will join with Muhammad (*Sal.*) as good people. God proved this state. Muhammad (*Sal.*) was given the false name of being a magician, but because he had all the 1,000 qualities which were given to the prophets, those who came before him bowed to his qualities and actions.

In spite of all this, Abu Jahil continued to do evil. He sent letters and messages to many kings, saying, "Muhammad is insulting and denying our ancestral gods. He calls the gods, which we have had for so long, false. Through magic, he is beginning to control everyone. The son of Abdullah and Amina is turning the city of Mecca upside down. He is trying to destroy everything. Therefore, you must help us restore our old religion and help us worship our ancestral gods again. You must help us!" Abu Jahil sent such messages to many kingdoms.

At that time, there was a king called Habib. He was a great emperor with many horses, many soldiers, and many warriors. He replied to Abu Jahil's request in a letter which said, "If Muhammad is trying to change our gods, I and my armies will come to help you fight him." And Habib did come to the city of Mecca with many battalions of horses, elephants, and camels. He brought battalions of foot soldiers, swordsmen, lancers, and archers. He brought all of them together in one army which was the size of ten immense armies. Abu Jahil and his forces welcomed Habib as a great king.

At that time, Muhammad (*Sal.*) was living in a hut. Habib sent a messenger and asked that Muhammad (*Sal.*) be brought before him. By this time, Abu Jahil had told Habib many degrading things about Muhammad (*Sal.*). Abu Talib [Muhammad's uncle] returned with the messenger and replied to those accusations: "O King, Muhammad is a son to me. After my brother's death I brought him up. He knows no magic. He knows no mantras. He knows no sorcery. He knows no bad qualities. He is called a prophet, and he *is* a prophet. He says that there is only one God, and that is true. He says that his God is everywhere, and he tells us to believe in Him. He has no words other than these. He has no magic, no mantra, and no sorcery. He does not want to kill anyone; he does not want to harm anyone. He has no thought of such things. If you want, you can call him and ask him the truth." Abu Talib said this to King Habib.

Then Habib said, "All right. I must ask him some questions." Again, Habib sent someone to bring Muhammad (*Sal.*) before him.

All the while Muhammad (*Sal.*) had been praying to Allah. He asked, "O God, what shall I do?" Only four of his followers ('Usman, 'Ali, Abu Bakr, and 'Umar [*Ral.*]) were with Muhammad (*Sal.*), but on the other side there were immense armies. And Muhammad (*Sal.*) said, "O God, save us from this. I do not know what I should do. It is Your *Rahmat*, Your grace alone which can protect us."

God sent Gabriel to Muhammad (*Sal.*). Gabriel said, "*As-salaamu 'alaikum,* Muhammad. Allah has told me to give His *salaams* to you. Allah has told me to say to you that you can go to King Habib happily and joyously. Allah has told me to say that you must not think you are alone, Muhammad. He will be sending all the heavenly beings with you to help you. Allah has said that He will send 3,000 angels to help you. This is what He told me to tell you." Gabriel told this to Muhammad (*Sal.*), gave his *salaams*, and left.

Now, Muhammad (*Sal.*) was ready to go to the king; but his wife, Khadijah, and everyone else were very sad. They prayed, "O God, save us. So many soldiers have come. So many armies have come. Please protect us. You must protect us."

As they were praying and asking for God's help, Gabriel came again, gave his *salaams*, and said, "We have all come to be with you. Come, it is time to go to the king." They went outside, and Gabriel told them to look at the sky. Gabriel called the angels from the heavens. "Muhammad, look at this." The angels were standing everywhere so that none of the earth could be seen. All the angels had swords and some were on horseback. When Muhammad (*Sal.*) looked at the sky, there were 3,000 angels in the heavens, each with 3,000 heads and 6,000 hands. And in each of these 6,000 hands were instruments of war. Gabriel said, "All of King Habib's armies will not be a match for even one angel. The whole city of Mecca will not be a match for even one angel. They cannot be compared.

Thus, will we all come with you."

Muhammad, the Messenger of Allah (*Sal.*), went forward. Where the angels on horseback were riding, there were no people to be seen, only dust. It was everywhere, covering everything. There were no people and no horses, but the entire sky was filled with 3,000 angels.

Abu Jahil had told his forces, "When Muhammad comes you should not stand up in respect. Do *not* get up and pay respect to him." But when Muhammad (*Sal.*) and his four followers came to meet them, as soon as they came to the doorstep, Abu Jahil stood up and bowed down. And then everyone got up in imitation.

King Habib also showed such respect. He came outside, gave Muhammad (*Sal.*) his hand, invited him in, and even offered Muhammad (*Sal.*) a seat on his own throne. He placed Muhammad (*Sal.*) in his seat and stood next to him. Then Muhammad (*Sal.*) asked him to sit down also. And King Habib said, "Muhammad, I must ask you some questions. I originally came with other intentions, but please do not worry because I have come with so many forces. If you can give satisfactory answers to what I ask, I will come on your path. I and all of my forces will become your followers. The question is: What proof is there that you are a prophet? The prophets who came before performed miracles and showed things to prove that they had come as prophets. They performed wonders, and because of this they were accepted as prophets. If we are to call you a prophet, then you must show us something appropriate to that state. If you show us something like that, then we will accept you as a prophet."

Muhammad (*Sal.*) said, "All right."

"Then what is your way?" he asked.

Muhammad (*Sal.*) answered, "I speak only the words of God. I have brought only the Qur'an. The Qur'an is the proof."

But the king said, "We cannot accept that as a wonder. There are three things I want you to do. If you can do those three things, we will accept you and your God. Then we will accept that you are a prophet."

Muhammad (*Sal.*) said, "Tell me what those three things are."

"First, at the time of the full moon, you must make it completely dark. There must be total darkness. Secondly, the full moon should reappear and become full again. You must first call the darkness, and then the full moon must come to dispel the darkness. Next, you must call the full moon, and it must come down to this assembly. It must come down and travel amidst the people and go into the *Ka'bah* [the cube-like building in the center of the mosque in Mecca]. It must go around the *Ka'bah* three times. You must stand on top of the mountain, and the moon must come to give *salaams* to you. The moon must call you a prophet. It must say this so that our ears can hear it. You must stand on that hill and the moon must go into your chest. It must come out in two pieces, one from each sleeve of your robe, and then the two halves must join again as one and go back into the sky. And from the sky the moon must say that Allah has sent you as the *Rasool* [the Messenger]. It must say the *Kalimah* [the remembrance of God] and the *salawāt* [a supplication for blessings and peace] and then disappear.

"First of all, you must make the night of the full moon become dark. Second, you must then make the full moon reappear and do the aforementioned things. Third, in my ancestry there was a child who was born because the mother and father had been praying for such a boon. That child was born as a piece of flesh. The people prayed so much, but the child was born as a piece of flesh. They went everywhere in order to get help. They meditated and they prayed, but it was all for nothing. Everyone said at that time, 'A prophet called Muhammad will come, and it is only through him that life can be given to this child. No one else can do this.' Because of this we have always kept this piece of flesh, preserving it until the prophet known as Muhammad should come. And you are named Muhammad. You must make this piece of flesh into a woman. You must do this."

Muhammad (*Sal.*) said, "Good." But he thought, "How can this ever be done?" And he went away.

The next day was to be the day of the full moon. All the Prophet's followers were crying; everyone was sad. The king had said that only if the miracles were performed would he accept the Prophet (*Sal.*). But some of the people in his armies were already saying to the forces of Abu Jahil, "He is the Prophet! If you hurt him, we will be on Muhammad's side, and we will kill Abu Jahil and his forces." Even at the time Habib was speaking to Muhammad (*Sal.*), half of King Habib's forces had this *Īmān*.

Meanwhile, Abu Jahil's forces were saying to him, "You told us not to get up and not to show respect to the Prophet (*Sal.*). Why did you get up first?" They created quite a commotion.

Abu Jahil answered them, "I did not get up. I did not get up! When Muhammad (*Sal.*) was coming in the door, through his sorcery two lions were at his sides. There was a lion on each of his shoulders. The lions were staring at me and getting ready to jump at me. I was frightened, and I got up. That is the only reason I got up. That is what he does through his sorcery."

This is the *wilāyat* of Allah. This is God's power. This is one *wilāyat* of Allah's 3,000 beautiful qualities of grace. Anyone who has Allah's grace will be protected like that. It will cause anyone who attacks you to go on the good path. Out of the three thousand qualities, this is one of the thousand which have been given to the prophets.

Muhammad (*Sal.*) stood on the hill and prayed. Then Allah's sound came to Muhammad (*Sal.*). Gabriel came to Muhammad (*Sal.*) and said, "O Muhammad, Allah has asked that I give you His *salaams*. Do not be afraid. Allah has said that He will do whatever you ask of Him."

So Muhammad (*Sal.*) prayed two *rak'ats* [a bow and

two prostrations], and then everyone—including King Habib, Abu Jahil, and all of their forces—came and filled the sides of the hill.

Soon the full moon arose and Muhammad (*Sal.*) said, "Let the moon disappear. Let it be dark."

At once Allah commanded the angel of darkness, "Out of all your darkness, send to the city of Mecca an amount of darkness equal in size to the eye of a needle." And that darkness came. The whole city of Mecca became dark as the sky was filled with darkness. The horses, their riders, and everyone were unable to see and fell down. Many people were trampled and crushed. The horses, the elephants, the camels, and the men were all running in fear, and many of them died.

Many blamed Abu Jahil, saying that the city of Mecca was being destroyed. "Abu Jahil has been taught by satan, and he came to destroy the city of Mecca! Why are you doing this? This land is being destroyed." They shouted and screamed like this.

After about forty-five minutes of darkness, King Habib accepted this sign and said, "Now call back the moon."

Muhammad (*Sal.*) lifted up his hands and spoke: "May the darkness be dispelled." The darkness receded and the full moon reappeared. Then Muhammad (*Sal.*) said, "Come to the center of the assembly, go into the *Ka'bah,* go three times around the *Ka'bah,* come into my chest and disappear there. Split into two, pass through the sleeves of my robe and join again into one. Then stand in the heavens. Say that Allah commands that this is the true Prophet and give the *salaam* and the *salawāt* in Allah's name. Stand in the heavens and say that this is the true Prophet, this is Allah's messenger, and that which Allah wishes to convey to the people has come to Muhammad as the Qur'an."

And it happened like that. The moon did these things. It was at this point that King Habib and his forces began to follow Muhammad (*Sal.*).

For the fulfillment of the third sign, they brought the piece of flesh before Muhammad (*Sal.*). Muhammad (*Sal.*) then said the *Bismin* and the *Kalimah*, and he put his hand over the piece of flesh. A woman as beautiful as the full moon appeared. King Habib asked the Prophet (*Sal.*) to take her for his wife. But the Prophet (*Sal.*) said, "She is like a child to me, like a sister to me." Then the Prophet (*Sal.*) told him to say the *Kalimah*, and the king and his forces complied.

Abu Jahil and his forces ran away, saying that King Habib had fallen subject to the sorcery of Muhammad (*Sal.*). "They will not help us," they said, and left.

Allah's powers exist in this state. To know the way to pray and to become *gnānis*, or people of wisdom, we must look first at the four religions. When one is born, he does not know *halaal* and *haraam*, or what is permissible and what is forbidden. He exists as a Hindu. When he is conceived, he is Islam and he is pure. When he takes form, he becomes Hindu; he comes out into the world, and he has all the desires and illusions. When he grows, he exists in the Hindu religion. Next, he enters the religion of Fire Worship, the religion of *Hanal*. He has hunger and illness and becomes subject to these. Next, he becomes subject to his own evil desires and those things which are of the third level, the religion of *Injeel*, or Christianity. Next, in the fourth level, he desires and becomes subject to physical visions, to the lights seen by his eyes, to sounds, to music, to the mind, to the senses, to smells, and to tastes. He becomes subject to women and material possessions and becomes controlled by them. These are the four religions.

Man is the four religions; they are within him. There is the section below the waist, relating to creation [Hinduism]; the section in the stomach, relating to hunger [Fire Worship]; the section in the chest, relating to the desires of the mind [Christianity]; and the section of the head, relating to the senses of perception [Islam]. Here in the section of the chest, he drinks milk from his mother. Here in the section of creation he is born. Here he gives food to the fire in the stomach. And here in the head, he is subject to physical visions, music, and similar things. He becomes subject to those things and is controlled by these four sections. He is controlled by these four paths. These are the four religions, the four kinds of studies, the four kinds of learning. First are the gods of form (earth). Next are the gods of fire (hunger). Third are the gods of evil desires. Fourth are the gods of light. Like this, there are four kinds of gods which are made in countless ways.

God made the four religions as four steps in order to teach wisdom to mankind. The four steps are *sharī'at, tarīqat, haqīqat,* and *ma'rifat*. This is the way one must worship inside. In *sharī'at* the evil desires, the forms, the mantras, the magic, the pride, the deception, the treachery, countless idols, demons, and ghosts are the objects of prayer. That is what is done in this section. *Sharī'at* means to see what is right and wrong (*shari*—right; *pilai*—wrong). One must see what is right and what is wrong. To understand what is right (*shari*) is *sharī'at*—to accept what is right, to get rid of what is wrong, to beat what is wrong, and to kill what is wrong. Everything wrong must be sent away and all evil must be cut away. What is right must be accepted. Then you go to the next level of *tarīqat*.

Imān must be made firm in *tarīqat*. After accepting what is right, that understanding must be made firm. We must accept God as the only thing which is right, and in His name we must become firm. This is *tarīqat*, and it exists within. That correct treasure, that correct meaning, must be merged with and prayed to. There is hunger, illness, desire, and old age. All these must be avoided, and God alone must be our food. Allah alone must be our food, and Allah alone must be accepted.

Patience, *saboor* [inner patience], *shukoor* [contentment], *tawakkal-Allāh* [absolute trust in God], and *Alhamdulillāh* [all praise belongs only to God]—with these five things, one must worship Allah. *Saboor* means that no matter what you get, you are patient. You are patient inside. No matter what comes to you, you have *shukoor*, you are content, you are satisfied. No matter what comes, you have *tawakkal-Allāh*, you give all responsibility to God. No matter what comes, say, "*Alhamdulillāh.*" That is how to worship God in *tarīqat*.

The next step is *haqīqat*. One's *Īmān* must be such that man is like a beautiful woman, and God is like a beautiful light. Merging with that light is *haqīqat*. Where one joins with God is *haqīqat*. Where the two embrace as one is *haqīqat*, or *Injeel*. That is Christianity. The religion is different, but this is inside.

The next step, *Furqān*, or Islam, is the state in which prayer has no day or night, where there is no dawn and no dusk, where there is no time, where one is always merged with God and praying in that state. There is no birth, no death, no destruction, no end.

Allah is One who has no destruction. Allah is One who has no end. He is One who has no color. He has no shape. He has no wife. He has no child. He has no sin. He has no end. He has no form, and He has no self-image. He has no selfishness. Allah has the 3,000 *wilāyats*, or powers of grace. If one is with Allah, then there is no specified *waqt*, or time for prayer. When one is with Allah, time does not exist. One who is like that has no age. He does not age. He has no death. One in that state prays while merged with God. That is known as *ma'rifat*. That is *Furqān*.

These four steps are the states of worship. If one can complete and transcend these four steps, then he comes to the station of *sūfīyat*. As he merges with Allah, that is *sūfīyat*. *Sūfīyat* is to speak without speaking. In the same way that firewood no longer exists after being burned and only the fire remains—in that way, one's world ends. His desire ends. His *nafs* [base desires] end. His birth and his existence end. His death ends. God alone is left. God

29

alone exists because he is merged with God. That state is called *sūfīyat*. There is *ma'rifat* and then *sūfīyat*. One must merge with that state.

This is true prayer and true worship. If one can completely achieve this state, then the 3,000 qualities of grace will be within him. Then the angels with 3,000 heads will be seen by him, standing behind him to protect him. Then he will see how many exist to help him and protect him. He will see the 3,000 qualities of grace and the 99 *wilāyats* of God. He will perform God's duties, God's actions, and God's service. He will be a *gnāni*, and he will have that wealth. He will be *Insān Kāmil*, or perfected man. When he reaches that state, when he reaches perfection, he will receive so much grace. He will receive all the grace in the four religions. He will receive the attributes of all four religions. He will receive the 1,000 qualities of grace given to the angels, he will receive the 1,000 qualities of grace given to the prophets, and he will receive the 999 qualities of grace given to the four religions. He will receive all this.

One who has the qualities of this grace, one who receives this grace, will be a true *gnāni*. He will be *Insān Kāmil*. He will be a true man. He will be a messenger of Allah. Man will be a very mysterious secret to Allah, and Allah will be a mysterious secret to man. That will be the state of mystery. Allah will be a mysterious secret within man. That secret is the story of Allah. Prayer means to see that story clearly. To establish that state is prayer. To establish that state is worship, and until that is established, there is no prayer. Everything that comes before is merely practice and training. Before this state is established, it is all just practice, or *palakkum*. When this state is established, it is *vanakkum*, or prayer.

Therefore, I have written this and drawn this picture to show each child. I have shown that this is what should exist within you. The mosques of prayer are like this. These are the mosques of prayer. This is what I have illustrated for you. I have drawn the inner meaning. It cannot be found outside somewhere; it exists within you. This is what must be transcended, step by step. One must climb up. You must try to accept the good qualities. If you come to that state, then you can reach true prayer.

May Allah give you the grace to do this. You must try to climb the steps within you. You must try to imbibe those good qualities. You must try to pray in this way. That will be exalted.

The world is capable of deceiving you. The world is a deception. Desire is a deception. Desire is something which can fascinate you. Attachments are deceptions that can fascinate you. Religions can deceive you. The earth and the lands are a deception. Money is a deception. Titles are a deception. Women are a deception. Material possessions are a deception. Honors are a deception, and learning is a deception. Like that, all of the things which are capable of fascinating you are trying to catch you. Hunger is a deception. Smells are a deception. What you see is a deception. Music is a deception. Taste is a deception. All of these things can catch you. They are *maya*, or illusion. It is with these things that satan will catch you. These are the weapons of satan. A child might be a deception. Blood-ties are a deception. Selfishness is a deception. It is through all these things that satan will try to catch us. These are satan's nets. These are satan's miracles. You must try to escape from them. As long as you are involved with all these miracles, you will not be living with Allah. You will live only with satan. You will be living in hell. You will be sharing in satan's share. It is after all these things are burned that we will live with God. It is after the firewood is burned that only the fire exists. That is true worship. These are ways to know what prayer is and then to pray. This is what we must know.

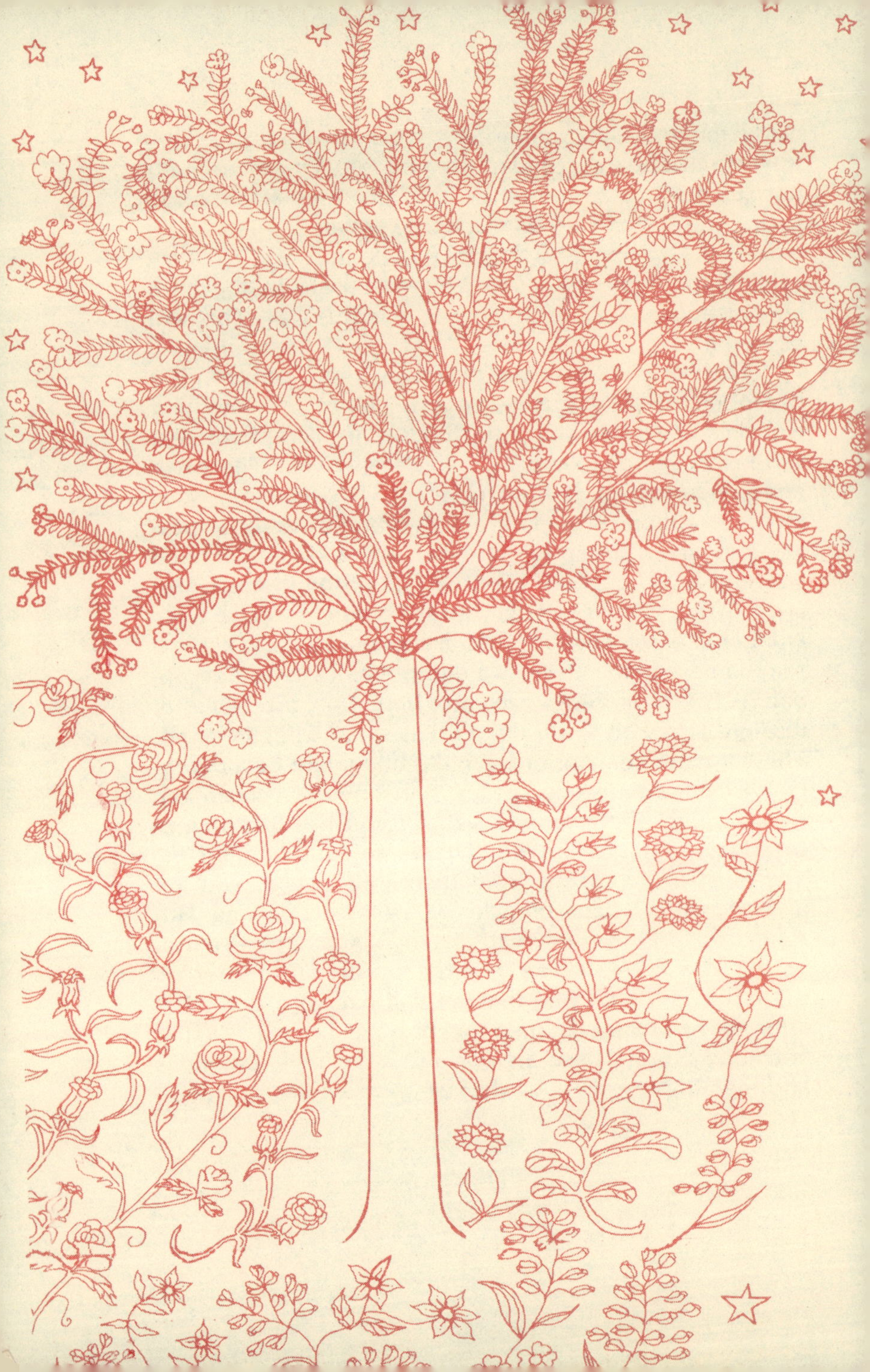

The Mystical Mirror

Bismillāhirahmāniraheem.
My love to the children. May God, the unfathomable ruler of grace who is limitless love, give you His grace and the wealth of His grace. May He give this to all of us. May His qualities and His actions come to exist within us. Just as God conducts His kingdom and just as He regards all lives, may we have those same qualities. May we do His duties and services in the same way that He does. May we do this with His grace.

Precious children, jeweled lights of my eyes, my own born created beings who are as the body within my body, may all of us join together as one and focus on our Father. May we live as one family in the world. May we worship the One God. May we bow down to Him, and may we disappear into His intention. God must give us this grace.

Precious children, jeweled lights within my eyes, all of us must join together as one. Not only must we meet together in bodily form, but we must join together in our hearts as well. We must live together and become one in our *qalbs*, and we must join together in what we see, in our thoughts, in our dreams, and in our intentions. We must exist without any differences at all. We must never see any separations in our actions or in our thoughts. We must reach this perfection.

Even in hunger, illness, and old age, may we live as one body and as one life. We must have the certitude to be aware of this unity. In the same way that God comforts all of creation, let us all establish this state within ourselves. This is the unity of the one family, one community, one heart, and one compassion. This is the love of God. May we establish this state.

We *must* establish this unity and make our hearts

perfect. Unity is not the way we commonly speak of it. It is not the way that we look at it. It is not the way we claim it to be. It is not the way that we do it. Our conduct, our thoughts, our speech, our hearts, our lives, and our bodies must be made one. In this way we must reach fullness in performing duty, and God's action must manifest. We must bring about that kind of heart within ourselves. Only if we develop that can we reach the state, the happiness, and the life of one family, the unity of brothers and sisters, and peace in each heart. Only then can we see tranquility. That will be perfection for us and completion for our hearts. That will be completion for the *qalb* and the completion of God's grace. If we make that completion of grace perfect and full, then we will see peace in the life of man. We will see the completeness of the one family, and we can know prayer to the One God. That will be perfect prayer. We will be a perfect family, perfect brothers and sisters. As we progress, we will realize the perfection found in such a life. Until this state comes, we will never see perfection.

Children, precious jeweled lights of my eyes, let us talk some more about this painting and about prayer. This is a picture of the mosque that must be built within us. We must build the place of prayer within us. There is only one God to whom worship belongs. Not to forget Him for even one second is prayer. Always being attached to Him is prayer. Not to forget Him in even one thought or one dream is prayer. Not to have evil thoughts, evil ideas, or differences will be the wealth in our lives. Not to hurt the heart of another, not to steal, murder, hit someone, or cause hurt to others is to have unity between brothers and sisters. To see the lives of others as we see our own lives, to perceive peace, to perceive equality, and to do duty will bring the unity between brothers and sisters. This is what will bring peace. To have good thoughts and good conduct will bring peace.

If prayer is to take place, we have to separate ourselves from evil. In prayer, we must be alone. Prayer is purity; it is not religious practice. Prayer means to be one pointed and to go up step by step.

To worship God inside, we must see that God has formed the four religions as four steps. There is *sharī'at*, *tarīqat*, *haqīqat*, and *ma'rifat*. We were born, we drank milk, we ate for our hunger and our illness, and we went to school. A few more years passed, we got married, and then we became old. All the while, we experienced desires and cravings, and we searched for materials possessions. Everything we see in life is *sharī'at*. It is all *sharī'at*. Our whole outer life exists as *sharī'at*. What we think of, what we search for, what we eat, what we imbibe, our searching for *halaal* and *haraam* [what is permissible and what is not permissible]—all that is *sharī'at*.

In this life of *sharī'at*, we must know what is right [*shari*] or wrong [*pilai*], what is *halaal*, what is *haraam*, what is *sifāt* [the manifestation of creation], what is *Zāt* [the essence of grace], what is *sharr* [evil], and what is *khair* [good]. All this must be understood. When we understand all this, we must accept only what is good, and we must avoid what is evil. We must avoid *sifāt* and accept the *Zāt*. We must avoid what is *haraam* and take only what is *halaal*. We must exist in such a state.

After we take what is right, and once we have determination and certitude of faith in God, then our state becomes *tarīqat*, which means we make our *Īmān* firm, and we place God in our hearts. The first step is *sharī'at*. After we have seen what is right and what is wrong, we must take what is right, have faith in God, and then build the proper mosque. First, we must realize the *sharī'at* of life. Next, in the second step we must realize the One to whom worship belongs, and we must build the mosque in which He is accepted. We must build that mosque and perform the prayer of *Īmān*. There is not one to whom worship is due other than *Allāhu ta'ālā*. For creation, for questioning, for the day of resurrection, for the prophets, for the lights of God, for this world and the next world, God is the one who judges. No one else can give that judgment. This is what we must accept with determination, and then we must build the mosque accordingly. That is *tarīqat*.

In *tarīqat* we have *shukoor* [contentment], saying, "*Alhamdulillāh*" [All praise belongs only to God]. If we receive food we say, "*Alhamdulillāh*." If we receive no food, we say, "*Alhamdulillāh!*" If we receive a beating, we say, "*Alhamdulillāh*." If we do not get beaten, we say, "*Alhamdulillāh!*" If a sadness comes to us, we say, "*Alhamdulillāh!*" If sadness does not come, we say, "*Alhamdulillāh!*" If we get a delicious rice dish or if we get only water, we say, "*Alhamdulillāh!*"

Patience, *saboor* [inner patience], *shukoor* [contentment], *tawakkal-Allāh* [absolute trust in God], and *Alhamdulillāh*—these are the prerequisites of *Īmān*. The second level of *tarīqat*, the state in which the certitude of *Īmān* exists within you, is the prerequisite to *Īmān-Islām*. As soon as *Īmān* becomes perfectly pure, as soon as your determination is correct, then the state of Islam, or light, will exist. You will become the light. '*Lām*' is light, the light of perfect purity. Light is pure. For that, purity, patience, *saboor*, *shukoor*, *tawakkal-Allāh*, and *Alhamdulillāh* are the pure food. They are the wage and the food given by God. At all times one must have *saboor*. If he gets food, he has *saboor*. If he gets less food, he has *shukoor*; he is still satisfied and contented. If he gets even less, he has *tawakkal-Allāh*, and if he gets even less than that, he says, "*Alhamdulillāh*." This is *Īmān-Islām*.

The first step is *sharī'at* and the second is *tarīqat*. First of all you must see what is right and what is wrong; only then can you transcend *sharī'at*. In *sharī'at*, you see the shadow forms within, and wherever you look outside you see the physical forms. That is the worship of idols. Inside, all the thoughts and intentions are shadow worship. What you see on the outside, everything, all of it, is idol worship—animal worship, monkey worship, donkey

37

worship. Secondly, to see this properly, to see that only God is right, to have the determination of faith, and to accept only God is the mosque built in the second step, the second mosque of *tarīqat*. Your *Īmān* must be made firm, and you must build that mosque.

In the second step (which is also the religion of Fire Worship), the fire of hell says, "Bring this, bring that. Bring me this, bring me that." It demands things.

But you must say to the fire, "*Alhamdulillāh*, you must have *shukoor*. Do not talk to me!"

"*Aiyo!*" it will cry. "I don't have this! I'm hungry! Please give me this, please give me that."

Again you must say, "Have *shukoor*, do not talk to me. I do not have time to talk to you."

It will cry, "Give me meat, give me fish."

But you must say, "Please do not talk to me. I do not have time to talk to you." You must say to the mind, "Do not talk to me." Having determined faith in Allah, say, "*Alhamdulillāh!*" Then continue to say, "You have been born on the earth and you consume the earth; you have been born in fire, and you consume fire; you have been born in fire, and you give room to fire; you have been born to air, and you give food to air; you have been born to *māya*, and you give food to *māya*; you have been born to the clouds, to the seven kinds of colors, and you desire the colors. Do you not have any peace? You only have the qualities of wandering. The oceans become lands. You run here, the air pushes you there, and the wind pushes you over there. Even the water does not stand still; it goes over there. The fire burns everything, the wind blows everything around, and the earth is trembling. Have those qualities not left you, O mind!"

You must have *saboor* and *shukoor* and tell the mind to have *saboor* and *shukoor*. To do that is *tarīqat*, to make *Īmān* firm. Tell the mind to have *shukoor* and make itself peaceful.

The third step is *haqīqat*, the religion of *Injeel*, or

Christianity. You must build this mosque. God is a beautiful, mystical thing. He is mystical and has a mysterious beauty. There is nothing which will not fall in love with Him when it sees His beauty. The heavenly beings, the angels, the celestial beings, the prophets, the lights of God, the earth, the sky, the lands, the nether worlds—all are submissive to His beauty. They all fall in love with Him when they see Him. When they see His beauty, when they see His qualities, His actions, His duty, and His miracles, they all fall in love. When they see the miracle of His compassionate qualities, the 3,000 qualities of His grace, His good thoughts, and His selfless duty, they all fall in love. When they see His compassionate gaze, when they perceive His sweet speech, when they see the beauty of the gaze of His eye, when they see the way that He carries us, so beautifully, so sweetly in our thoughts and in our dreams, in the way that He embraces us and gives us milk, when they see His state of love, everyone will fall in love with His beauty. *Haqīqat* is to merge (*ayikkiya*) with that Beautiful One.

Haqīqat means to merge with Him, to say, "I am a slave to Your beauty. Your beauty alone do I want. I want Your bliss. I do not see anything other than You. There is no beauty other than Your beauty. There are no qualities other than Your qualities. I have seen no compassion other than Yours. I have seen no action other than Your action. There is no love comparable to Your state of love. There is no wealth other than Your unfathomable qualities of grace. There is no one else who can act with Your perfect actions. O God, there is no god other than You. I love You alone. I must merge with You."

Build that mosque! These spirits—this pure spirit, this spirit and that spirit—they are all just creations, and they will all change. He alone is the unchanging Beautiful One. He is the undiminishing Beautiful One. He is the indestructible Beautiful One. His mystery alone is mystery. His miracle alone is the true miracle. To be in love with the Beloved One, to be blissful with Him, to merge with Him, and to join with Him is *haqīqat*. That is Christianity. We are speaking of the state of prayer, not the religion. It is not the religion. There are four steps of prayer which are the four religions: *Zaboor*, *Jabrāt*, *Injeel*, and *Furqān*. But there is only one God to whom worship belongs, and there are these four steps for us to come to accept Him. It is in the third step that one merges with God. That is Christianity.

The next step is *Furqān*. *Furqān* is light, the light which contains no day and no night. It has no darkness. It is also called the state of *ma'rifat*. In a place without darkness, there is no time and there are no seasons. In a place without time, there is no age. In a place where there is no aging, there is no death. In a place where there is no death, there is no birth. In a place where there is no birth and death, there is no time of questioning. In a place where there is no questioning, there is no judgment. And in a place without judgment, one can eternally exist. That is *ma'rifat*, where the ten are transcended. *Furqān* means there is no day and no night, only the light of Allah's seven causal signs.

The meaning of the seven causal signs is as follows: The Arabic alphabet consists only of consonants. These are accompanied with diacritical marks which can either identify the consonant, indicate it is vowelless, add a vowel to the consonant, or double the consonant. For example, if the letter *alif* ( ) is by itself it has no sound; if a *fathah* is placed above it ( ), the sound becomes 'ah'; if a *kasrah* is placed below it ( ), the sound becomes 'ee'; and if you place a *dammah* above the *alif* ( ), the sound becomes 'oooh'. A *maddah* can be placed with the *fathah*, *kasrah*, or *dammah* to lengthen the sound of the vowel. A *shaddah* placed above a letter ( ) indicates that it is doubled; and a *sukoon* ( ) indicates that it is vowelless. A *nuqat* placed above or below a letter distinguishes certain consonants from others.

Like these seven diacritical marks, there are seven causal signs in man: two eyes, two ears, two nostrils, and one mouth. It is through these seven that things can be perceived. Man exists as the form of the Qur'an. He has been formed out of the 28 letters which form the Qur'an. *Sūratul-Fātihah* is the opening chapter of the Qur'an. *Sūrah* [chapter] also means 'form' or 'body', and in Tamil *'partiya'* (which sounds like *fātihah*) means, "Have you seen?" Therefore, *Sūratul-Fātihah* can be understood as 'the inner form of man', or "Have you seen your true form?" And *Sūratul-Insān* can also be understood as 'the inner form of man'.

When we look at this in depth, we see that we must analyze with these seven sounds, these seven essences, these seven diacritical marks. *Insān*, or man, is the Qur'an. Allah's mystery exists within him. The mystery of *Insān* and the mystery of Allah dwell in the same place. These are very mystical things. Everything exists within man. The 6,666 verses of the Qur'an are within man. There is the *Sūratul-Fātihah*, the *Sūratul-Qur'ān*, *Sūratu Yā Sīn*, the *Sūratul-Baqarah*, and the *Sūratur-Rahmān*; we must understand all of them. There are also so many *hadīsz* [traditional stories of Islam] within man. This is the mystical wisdom. This mysterious wisdom is the Qur'an. But not everything you look at is the Qur'an. Not all the prayers you perform can be called prayer. The state of worship which knows what true prayer is, the state which has no day and no night, becomes the Qur'an.

That Qur'an must be given sound. These are the seven causal signs (two eyes, two ears, two nostrils, and a mouth), the seven diacritical marks. It is with these essences, with these things, that God's mystery must be given sound. This is what gives sound to the Qur'an. In the *āyats* [verses] of the Qur'an, mystical wisdom explains what sound has to come to which perception. That is the mystery. When you open this Qur'an and read, mystical wisdom will explain where each mark is to be placed.

Whether it is to be a *fathah* or *kasrah* or *dammah* or *shaddah*. Whether the mark should come on the letter *'lām'*, the letter *'meem'*, the letter *'rāy'*, or the letter *'they'*. Then you can know which sound must be given. Likewise, sound must then be given to *Sūratul-Insān*, to the inner form of man. In Tamil, *saddu* means life or essence; this is the 'sound' that must be given. It is only after we know these seven essences, it is after we know these seven causal signs, that the state of *Furqān*, or *ma'rifat*, occurs. This prayer of *ma'rifat* is the fourth step.

Next is *sūfīyat*, the place where one disappears into Allah. How does the disappearing take place? Allah is the mysterious treasure; He is the miracle. Actually, God is not a miracle, but a mirror. A miracle simply means magic tricks, and God is not that kind of miracle. He is a mirror. Everyone who goes before that mirror sees his own face. All the worlds can be seen in that mirror. Anyone who looks will see himself. Everyone can see his own *sūrat*, his own form, his own actions, his act, his shape, and his clothing. He can see whatever he does, he can see whatever he wants. That is the miracle mirror. That miracle and that prayer is *sūfīyat*.

What is prayer? It is the mercury which is bonded to the mirror. Devotion [*'ibādat*] is how you can bow to Allah. That is how you can bond yourself to God. That is prayer. That is the mercury. And as soon as that place is touched, that is the miracle mercury of the mirror.

Are the two separate? No. When glass and mercury are bonded, the mirror is formed. Then the mirror becomes crystal, a crystal mirror. Then Allah, prayer, and *Insān* will be one. At the time when they work together, the miracle occurs. Prayer is the mercury which must bond with Him. When that state is established, prayer exists. That is *toluhay*, that is *'ibādat*, that is purity, that is white. That is the mirror into which we must look, that is the miracle, and that is mystical. It is God's mystical mirror, a mystery.

It is in this way that we must control our hearts. We must control our qualities, and we must control our actions. We must know this mosque, we must know this state of worship, and we must build these four steps here, inside. God's house must exist in the flower garden. It must be built here, inside. In this prayer, we must go up step by step, and we must transcend the four religions. We must transcend the four stories. We must transcend the four steps and go to God in the way that mercury is bonded to the mirror. Our prayer must be bonded to Him. That bonding is prayer. Until that state is established, prayer does not exist. Before that state is established, our prayers will be like throwing a stone at a mountain of rock. The stone will only return; it will only come back to us.

What we are doing today is just practice. It is the practice which has been done throughout our ancestry; it is what our fathers did, what our grandfathers did, what our great-grandfathers did, what they did in this religion, what they did in that religion. These are just practices. They are supermarket practices. When you take a child to the supermarket it says, "Buy me this, buy me that. Buy me this, mommy. Buy me that, mommy. Buy me this. Buy me toys, buy me candy, buy me cookies, buy me a cookie." This is how we try to go to God. We want miracles from our prayers; we pray for miracles. We say, "O God, buy me this in the supermarket of the world. Buy me that. O God, give me the love of women, buy me that. O God, I have to pass that test, I am taking a test, make me pass that exam. O God, give me money, give me a house. O God, give me this, give me that." Those things are not miracles; it is just supermarket work. If you go to God to ask for these things, it will only be supermarket work.

Prayer is an entirely different thing. Supermarket work will not be prayer. This is what we did when we were babies, when we asked our fathers and mothers for things in the supermarket. If we go to God, we say, "Kill him, break his leg, make him fall. He is opposing me, he is bad, he has done this to me, he has done that to me. O God, destroy his eyes." Is that what God does? Is God a torturer? Is God a murderer? Is God a killer? Is God a businessman? No. Is God a broker? Is God a pimp who will give you women? Is God a pimp who stands in front of a prostitute's house? This is not what God does. This is what we do while we are ignorant. These are the practices we practice in the time of ignorance.

It is only after you truly know what prayer is, that prayer can take place. To know God with certitude, is prayer. And then after you know this, you must have Īmān. All idols are opposite to God. Man has made so many tens of millions of idols. Is that God? Are those animals gods? Is God a pig? Is God a dog? Is God a cat? You have to understand who God is, and you must have absolute Īmān and belief in Him. Know God and have Īmān! You must know what God is and then pray. That becomes the worship of the unfathomable ruler of grace, the One who is undiminishing love. To establish that state is prayer. "And then," Allah has said, "you will know the truth." That is what Allah has said. But what we do now is supermarket work. We go to God and ask for things. This is not prayer.

True prayer is like mercury on a mirror. True prayer is like mercury bonded to a mirror. Devotion must bond itself to Him. Our devotion, our prayer, and our worship has to bond with light. It must bond itself to the mirror; it must become one. That state is the state of prayer. If that state does not exist, then prayer does not exist.

We must think of this, children. Prayer is like this, and wisdom is like this. To be attached to God, to be connected to God, to be tied to God is like this. That state shows us the place from which we have to pray. We have to know this. Each child must touch this and follow this. Precious children, jeweled lights of my eyes, only then can we reach the place which we must reach. Then we can obtain the state which we must obtain. Then we can merge with the One with whom we must merge. Then we can reach that state. Each child must realize this. Please try to do this; this will be good. This is the true path, not a path of business. This is the direct path which we must know. My love and my greetings to you. My *salaams* to all of you. *As-salaamu 'alaikum* [May the peace of God be upon you].

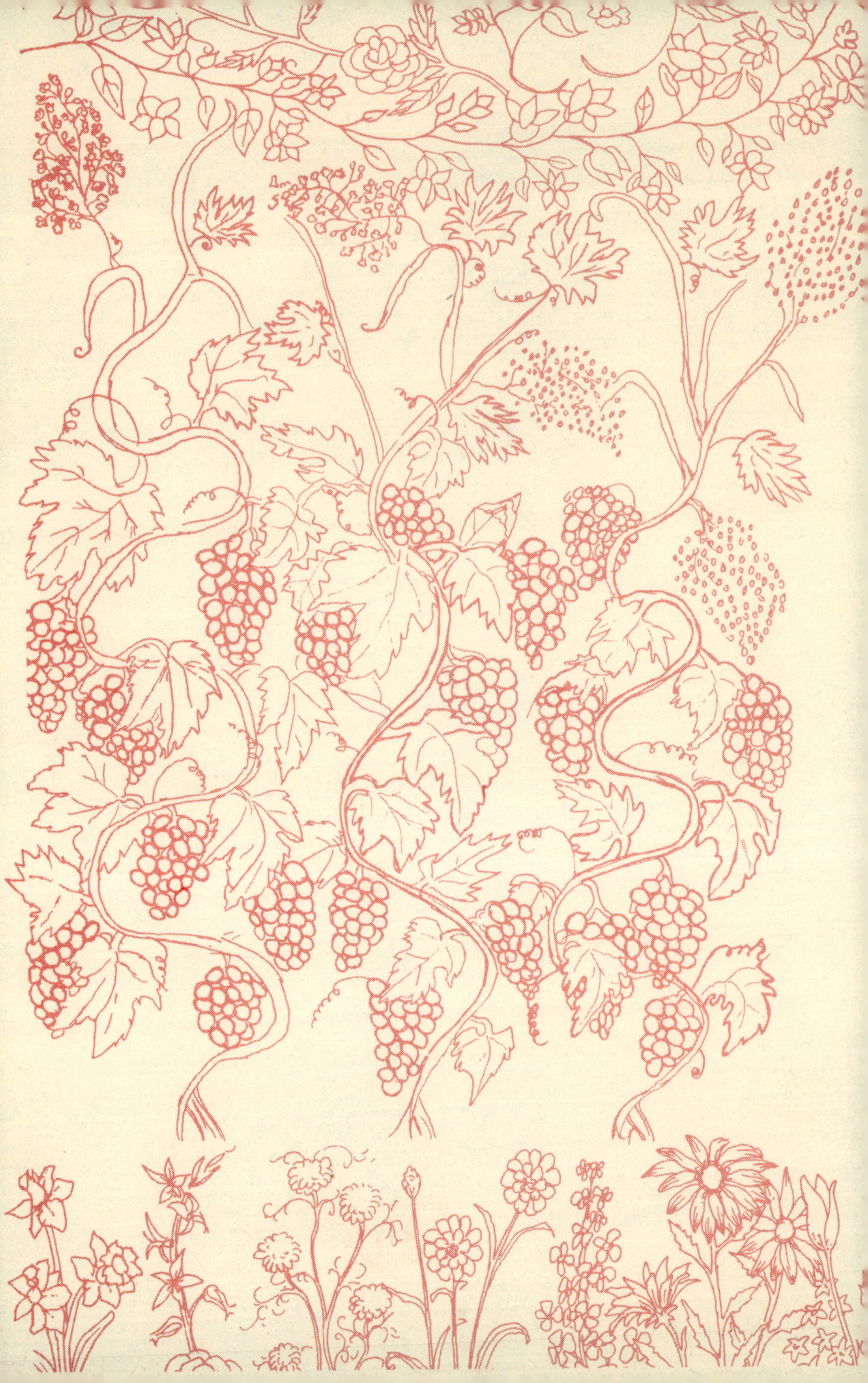

Glossary and Index

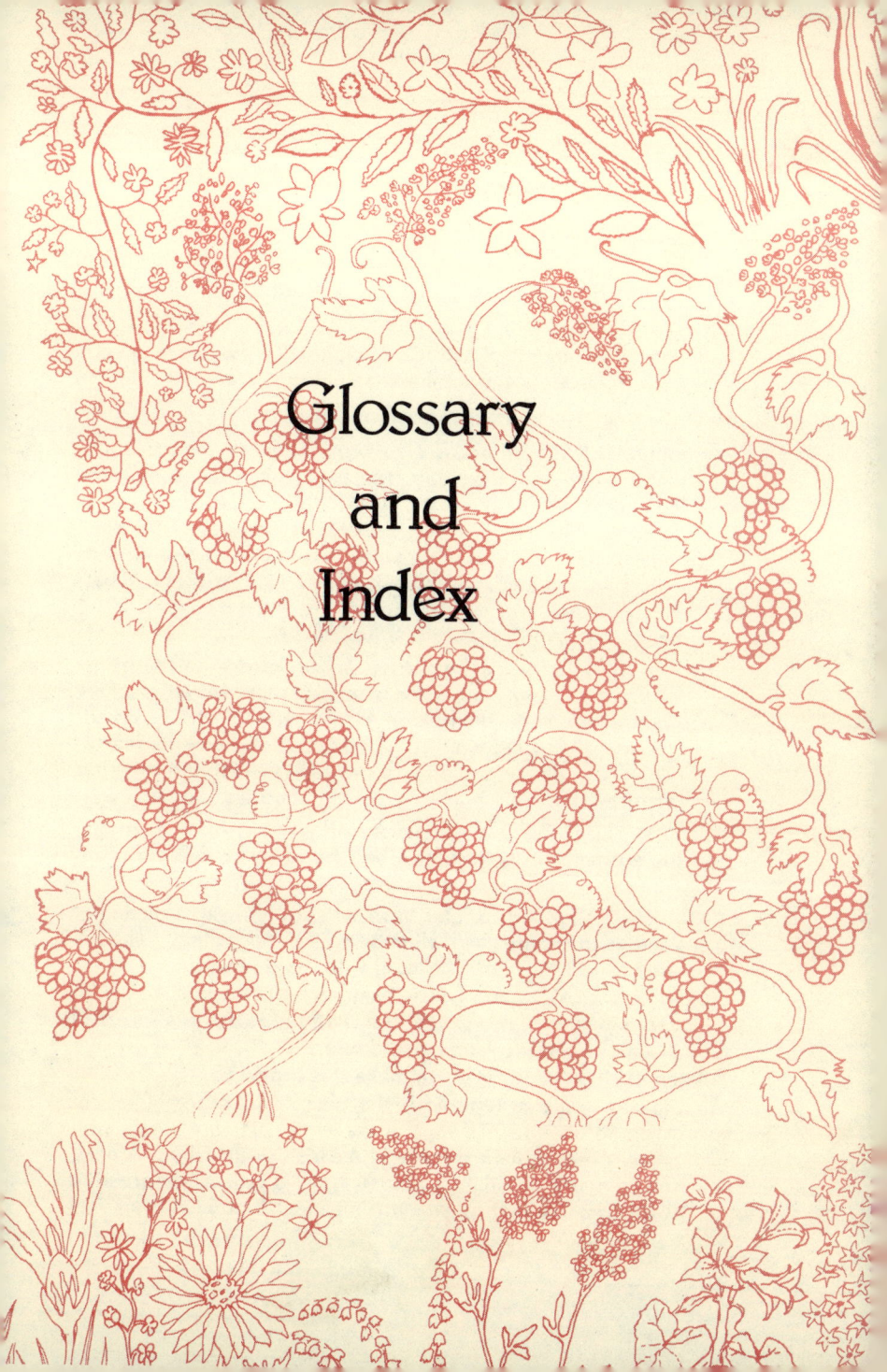

(A) *indicates an Arabic word.* (T) *indicates Tamil.*

agnānam (T)   Ignorance; worldly or materialistic wisdom; speech from the level of the intellect. See also: *Gnānam.*

aiyo! (T)   An exclamatory expression, "Oh no!"

Alhamdulillāh (A)   All praise is to You. The glory and greatness that deserve praise is Allah. You are the One responsible for the appearance of all creations. Whatever appears, whatever perishes, whatever receives benefit or loss—all is Yours. I have surrendered everything into Your hands. I remain with hands outstretched, spread out, empty, and helpless. Whatever is happening and whatever is going to happen is all Yours. Lit.: All praise is to and of Allah!

alif, lām, meem, hey, dāl (A)   Five Arabic letters. In the transformed man of wisdom, these letters are represented as: *alif*—Allah; *lām*—*Noor*, the light of wisdom; *meem*—Muhammad. *Hey* and *dāl* correspond to the body of five elements [earth, fire, water, air, and ether], to the *sirr* [secret] and the *sifāt* [manifestations of creations], and to mind and desire.

Allāh (A)   God; the One who is beyond comparison or example; the eternal, effulgent One; the One of overpowering effulgence.

Allāhu (A)   Allah and *Allāhu* have virtually the same meaning. Allah is the name used when one talks about Him. *Allāhu* is used to call for Him. It is said with more feeling.

Allāhu ta'ālā (A)   God, Most Exalted. *Allāhu:* the beautiful undiminishing One. *Ta'ālā:* the One who exists in all lives in a state of humility and exaltedness.

Āmeen (A)   So be it. May He make this complete.

As-salaamu 'alaikum (A)   May the peace and peacefulness of Allah be upon us. To say "*As-salaamu 'alaikum*" is to welcome someone with respect. It means, "I am Islam. Among the creations of Allah, I am Islam." To return the greeting with "*Wa 'alaikumus-salaam*" means, "I am also Islam. By the grace of Allah, I am also Islam. We are one family of Islam. We are all the children of Adam. We live in the same place. We greet all with respect and love." This is a greeting of love.

As-salaamu 'alaikum, wa 'alaikumus-salaam. One heart embraces the other with love and greets with respect and honor. Both hearts are one. *Wa 'alaikumus-salaam.* I am also Islam. This is Allah's word. This is a word from Allah that reunites all in Islam. If one gives salutation, you must always return the salutation. Otherwise, you may incur a serious debt.

With this salutation you are acknowledging: 1) all of everything that was created is Islam; 2) all of mankind, every fetus born is Islam; 3) God has said, "O Muhammad, I would not have created anything without you"; and 4) "Everything I have created through you is perfect purity and purity is Islam."

ayikkiya (T) Unity with Allah; the state where the heart comes into unity with Allah. Bawa uses this Tamil word to give meaning to the Arabic word *haqīqat* [the third step of spiritual ascendance, or the beginning of communication with God].

Bismillāhirahmāniraheem (A) In the name of God, Most Merciful, Most Compassionate.

Bismillāh: Allah, the first and the last; the One in the beginning but without a beginning. He is the One who is the cause for creation and for the absence of creation, the cause for the beginning and for the beginningless. He is the One who is completeness.

Ar-Rahmān: He is the King, the Compassionate One, and the Beneficent One. He is the One who protects all creations and gives them nourishment. He looks after them, gives them love, takes them unto Himself, and comforts them. He gives them food, houses, property, and everything within Himself. He holds His creations within Himself and protects them. He is the One who reigns with justice.

Ar-Raheem: He is the One who redeems, the One who protects us from evil, the One who preserves and confers eternal bliss. No matter what we may do, He has the quality of forgiving us and accepting us back. He is the Tolerant One who forgives all the faults we have committed. He is the Savior. On the day of judgment, on the day of inquiry, and on all days since the beginning, He protects and brings His creations back unto Himself.

Bismin (A)   The shortened form of *Bismillāhirahmāniraheem*. To give the full meaning of *Bismin* would require 1,000 pages. All God's treasures [*daulat*] and all His wealth begin with the *Bismin*. The beginning of every one of His creations is from the *Bismin*. For all lives, for all the grace, for all the miracles [*siddhis*] and all the powers, God has made the *Bismin* the commander. This is the first thing that was written on His throne [*dhahūt*].

The *Bismin* is the beginning for all beginnings. We must realize this, and one must say it firmly with one's heart. It is a word which is endowed with much beauty and a great, exalted state. Of all His names, this is a word of beauty. See also: *Bismillāhirahmāniraheem*.

dammah (A)   An Arabic diacritical mark which gives the sound 'u' (like the 'o' in the word 'to') to the letter over which it is written.

daulat (A)   This has two meanings: one is the wealth of the world [*dunyā*], and the other is the wealth of Allah's grace. That wealth of Allah is the wealth of divine knowledge ['*Ilm*] and the wealth of perfect *Imān* [absolute faith, certitude, and determination]. If one were to fill his heart with only that limitless wealth of Allah's grace, then that would be the *daulat* of limitless completeness and perfect purity for the three worlds of *awwal* [the beginning of creation], *dunyā* [this world], and *ākhir* [the hereafter].

fathah (A)   Arabic diacritical mark which denotes the vowel 'a'.

Fikr (A)   Contemplation of God or one of His qualities.

There are 6,666 kinds of *Zikr* [remembrance of God]. *Zikr* means prayer that is heard and recited. This includes singing, reciting in the heart, reciting outwardly, or reciting silently. *Salaam*, *salawāt*, *Zikr*, and *Fikr* are different names given to these prayers. There are the various levels of *Zikr*. At the first level, the remembrance of God is from one's awareness within the innermost heart [*qalb*]. The *Zikr* within *Zikr* is done with feeling from within the heart.

Secondly, when prayer is taken further within and is said by the soul [*Rūh*], that is *Fikr*.

And thirdly, when the soul, wisdom, and the *Noor* [the resplendence of Allah] join together and recite *Fikr* at the same time, when all three are in one station in the remembrance of God, that is the devotion ['ibādat] of the *Noor*, *'Ibādatuz-Zikr*. Each stage has a subtly different meaning. *'Ibādat* is the *Fikr* within *Fikr*. When one gets to the stage of the *Noor*, wisdom, and the soul and prays without a sound, that is *sūfīyat*. That is prayer. That prayer does not come from the breath but is in connection with the soul, wisdom, and the *Noor*. That is the triple flame. When all three rays go together and become connected to God, that is *Zikrul-Fikr*.

There is *Zikr*, *Zikr* within *Zikr*, *Fikr* within *Zikr*, *Fikr* within *Fikr*, *Noor* within *Fikr*, and Allah within *Noor*. These are the various levels of *Zikr*. There are 6,666 different kinds of prayers, chanting and various other things. There are so many branches and divisions. These are all parts and different levels of prayer to God. See also: *Zikr*.

Furqān (A) Islam. See also: *Zaboor*, *Jabrāt*, *Injeel*, and *Furqān*.

Gabriel or Jibrīl (A) The angel who brings the revelations of Allah and through whom Allah conveyed the Qur'an to Prophet Muhammad (*Sal.*).

Gnānam (T) Divine Analytic Wisdom; *Pahuth-Arivu*. Allah has placed within the body of man the wealth of all the 18,000 universes. Within his hands man holds hell and heaven, good and evil [*khair* and *sharr*], the secret and the manifestations [*sirr* and *sifāt*], the essence and the manifestations [*Zāt* and *sifāt*], and that which is forbidden and that which is permissible [*haraam* and *halaal*]. Allah has placed within man the wealth of the world, of heaven and hell; the wealth of the *nafs* [base desires]; the wealth of satan; the wealth which desires desire; the treasure which earth desires, which water desires, which fire desires, or which the air and the spirits desire; and the treasures which illusion [*māya*] desires. If man can throw away all these treasures and take within him only the treasure called Allah and His qualities, His actions, His conduct and behavior; if he makes Allah the only treasure and completeness for him, that is the state of *Gnānam*. What treasure is there other than Allah? All the rest is *agnānam* [ignorance] and *poignānam* [false wisdom]. False wisdom, or *poignānam*, is the *gnānam* of darkness, the words which one speaks in the torpor and intoxication of darkness. *Agnānam* is the *gnānam* of the world, the speech from the intellect. *Vingnānam* [scientific wisdom] is the explanation given by the subtle intellect. *Meignānam* is to know and understand.

Meignānam is from Allah's words; it is to know and understand through Allah's word, and to eliminate all that is evil. It is to know that there is no treasure other than God. *Meignānam* is to know that everything other than God is perishable and destructible and to discard those things.

gnāni (T)   A man of wisdom; one who has *Gnānam*; one who has received the qualities and wisdom of God by surrendering to God, and, having received these, lives in a state of peace and equality where he sees all lives as equal; one who has attained the state of peace.

hadīsz (A)   In Islam, a traditional story of the prophets. The words or commands of Allah were received by Prophet Muhammad (*Sal.*) and other prophets and were conveyed and demonstrated to the people. These words were given directly from Allah to the prophets without Gabriel as an intermediary. For example, when God asked Abraham to sacrifice his son, Ishmael, Allah spoke directly to Abraham. When Moses received the Ten Commandments on Mt. Sinai, Allah spoke directly. When Prophet Jonah asked God to destroy the people of his country, God spoke directly. The words that God spoke directly, apart from the other words that He conveyed through Gabriel, are called *hadīsz*.

halaal (A)   Those things that are permissible or lawful according to the commands of God and conform to the word of God, relating both to food and to knowledge [*'Ilm*].

Hanal (T)   The second religion or step; Fire Worship; the equivalent of *Jabrāt*. See also: *Zaboor, Jabrāt, Injeel,* and *Furqān*.

haqīqat (A)   The third step of spiritual ascendance; the realization of Divinity and the beginning of communication with God. See also: *sharī'at*.

haraam (A)   That which is forbidden by truth, forbidden by justice, forbidden by the warnings or commands of God. For those who are on the straight path, *haraam* means all the evil things that can be obstacles to them, the dangers that can obstruct them, and the actions and the food that can block them on the straight path.

'ibādat (A)   Prayer; worship and service to the One God.

In the many languages there are many common words such as prayer, *pūjās*, meditation, and worship. In Arabic the term is *'ibādat*. But true *'ibādat* is when the heart melts like molten wax and is in prayer to the One God. Only that state can truly be called prayer.

Īmān (A) Absolute and complete and unshakable faith, certitude, and determination that God alone exists; the complete acceptance by the heart that God is One. See also: *saboor*, for the five prefaces to *Īmān*.

Īmān-Islām (A) The state of the spotlessly pure heart which contains Allah's Holy Qur'an, His divine radiance, His divine wisdom, His truth, His prophets, His angels, and His laws. The pure heart which, having cut away all evil, takes on the power of that courageous determination called faith and stands shining in the resplendence of Allah. When that resplendence of Allah is seen as the completeness in the heart of man, then that is *Īmān-Islām*. When the complete unshakable faith of the heart is directed toward the One who is completeness; when that completeness is made to merge with the One who is completeness; when that heart communes with the One who is completeness, trusts only in Him, and worships Him, accepting only Him and nothing else, accepting Him as the only perfection and the only One worthy of worship—that is *Īmān-Islām*.

Injeel (A) Christianity. See also: *Zaboor, Jabrāt, Injeel,* and *Furqān*.

Insān (A) True man; a true human being; the true form of man: the form of Allah's qualities, actions, conduct, behavior, and virtues. An *Insān* is one who has the completeness of this form, who has filled himself with these qualities.

Insān Kāmil (A) A perfected, God-realized being. One who has made Allah his only wealth, cutting away all the wealth of the world and the wealth sought by the mind. One who has acquired God's qualities, performs his own actions accordingly, and contains himself within those qualities.

Islām (A) Spotless purity; the state of absolute purity. To accept the commands of God, His qualities, and His actions; to establish that state within oneself; to cut away the desire called *'ishq*; to accept Him and know Him without the slightest doubt, and then to worship Him, is Islam. To accept *Lā ilāha ill Allāhu* [There is no God other than Allah] with certitude, to strengthen one's *Īmān* [absolute faith, certitude, and determination] and to affirm this *Kalimah*—that is the state of Islam. Also: the religion or creed of Islam.

Jabrāt (A) Fire Worship. See also: *Zaboor, Jabrāt, Injeel,* and *Furqān*.

jinn (A)   A genie, a fairy, a being created from fire.

Ka'bah (A)   In Islam, the *Ka'bah* is the most important shrine for worship. On the path of *sharī'at* [the first step of spiritual ascendance], one of the five obligations [*fardhs*] is the pilgrimage [*hajj*] to the *Ka'bah*.

Another meaning: The place from which the earlier prophets and the final prophet, Muhammad (*Sal.*), prayed to Allah. The *Ka'bah* is the place from which a true man [*Insān*] meets Allah face to face; it is the heart, the original source of prayer. The prayers from a heart which has not developed to the right state will never be fulfilled. Whoever brings his heart to that state of perfection and prays to God from that heart will be praying from the *Ka'bah*. But as long as the heart is not in that state, that prayer will never reach fulfillment, no matter from where one prays.

Allāhu ta'ālā, God Almighty, dwells within every heart. He is the only One who knows and understands each heart and gives each one its needs. He does not look at the body or the wealth of the world. He looks only at the heart and at the state of *Īmān* [absolute faith, certitude, and determination]. If the perfectly pure state of *Īmān* is established within the heart, then God dwells within such a heart. To know God without the slightest doubt, to see God and worship Him face to face, and to hand over that heart in complete surrender—in that state the heart becomes the exalted *Ka'bah* which is acceptable to God.

Kalimah (A)   *Lā ilāha ill Allāhu:* There is nothing other than You, O God. Only You are Allah. The recitation or remembrance of God which cuts away the influence of the five elements (earth, fire, water, air, and ether), washes away all the karma that has accumulated from the very beginning until now, and beautifies and dispels the darkness of the heart and makes it resplend. The *Kalimah* washes the body and the heart of man and makes them pure, makes his wisdom emerge, and impels that wisdom to know the self and God.

karma (T)   The inherited qualities formed at the time of conception; the qualities of the essences of the five elements; the qualities of the mind; the qualities of the connection to hell; the qualities and actions of the seventeen *purānas* which are: the six qualities of arrogance, karma, *māya* [illusion]; *tārahan, singhan,* and *sūran* [the three sons of *māya*]; the six intrinsic evils of lust, anger, greed, attachment, bigotry, and envy; and the five acquired evils of intoxication, desire, theft, falsehood, and murder.

kasrah (A) An Arabic diacritical mark which gives the sound 'e' as in 'be' to the letter under which it is written.

khair (A) That which is right or good; that which is acceptable to wisdom and to Allah; as opposed to *sharr*, that which is evil or bad.

Kursī (A) The gnostic eye; the eye of light; the center of the forehead where the light of Allah's *Noor* [resplendence] was impressed on Adam's forehead. Lit.: the seat of the resplendence of Allah.

lām (A) The Arabic letter (ل) which correlates to the English consonant 'l'. In the transformed man of wisdom, *lām* represents the *Noor* [the resplendence of Allah]. See also: *alif*.

maddah (A) An Arabic diacritical mark which lengthens the vowel over which it is written. *Maddah* literally means lengthening.

mantra (T) An incantation or formula; the recitation of a magic word or set of words; sounds imbued with force or energy through constant repetition, but limited to the five elements. (The *Kalimah* is not a mantra.)

ma'rifat (A) The fourth step of spiritual ascendance; the state of merging with God. See also: *sharī'at*.

māya (T) Illusion; the unreality of the visible world; the glitters seen in the darkness of illusion; the 105 million glitters seen in the darkness of the mind which result in 105 million rebirths; an energy [*sakti*] that can take many, many millions of hypnotic forms. If man tries to grasp these forms with his intellect, he will be able to see a form; but he cannot catch it, for it will take on yet a different form. *Māya* is an energy which takes on various shapes, makes man forfeit his wisdom, and makes him confused and hypnotized into a state of torpor.

meem (A) The Arabic letter (م) which correlates to the English consonant 'm'. In the transformed man of wisdom, *meem* represents Muhammad. The shape of *meem* is like a sperm cell and from this comes the *nuqat* or dot which is the form of the world. See also: *alif*.

Muhammad (A) The effulgent face of God's light; the brilliant heart of grace; the essence of God; the messenger of Allah who emanates from Allah; the *Noor* or effulgence of Allah; the beauty of God's qualities that entrances everything in creation. There are three *meems* in Muhammad, and one is this beauty.

The common meaning for Muhammad is the last one of the line of prophets. But, in truth, Allah has said, "O Muhammad, I would not have created anything without you." That same beauty called *meem*, which came at the beginning, also comes at the end as the beauty of Muhammad. If something was not there at the beginning, it could not come at the end. See also: *meem*.

nafs or nafs ammārah (A)   The seven kinds of selfish desires. That is, desires meant to satisfy one's own pleasure and comfort. All the thoughts are contained within the *ammārah*. *Ammārah* is like the mother while the *nafs* are like the children. Lit.: person or spirit.

Noor (A)   The resplendence of Allah; the plenitude of the light of Allah; the completeness of Allah's qualities. When the plenitude of Allah's qualities and Allah's beauty becomes one and resplends as one, that is the *Noor*.

nuqat (A)   Dots (used in text to mean a singular dot); a diacritical mark placed over or under certain Arabic letters to differentiate one from another.

palakkum (T)   Practice.

Partiyā? (T)   Lit.: Have you seen? Bawa frequently puns on the Tamil word *partiyā* and the Arabic *Sūratul-Fātihah*. *Sūrat* said with two different Arabic pronunciations of the letter 's' can be 'chapter' or 'form'. The literal meaning of *Sūratul-Fātihah* is 'the opening chapter of the Qur'an', but Bawa also explains it as 'the inner form of man'. To further this interpretation: using the similar sounding Tamil word, *Sūratul-Partiyā*, means, "Have you looked at your inner form?" By mixing the Tamil and Arabic languages with this pun, Bawa is differentiating between the outer Qur'an and the Qur'an within the form of man.

pilai (T)   Wrong; as opposed to *shari*.

pūjā (T)   Ritual devotion. Performing *pūjā* is the offering of worship to the thoughts and demons that arise in one's mind; making a form of those thoughts and demons and worshiping them within and without; and offering flowers, fruits, and various things to the deities of the mind. Those deities live in darkness, and the people light candles for them and ask them to come out. But then they ask those deities to provide them with light! To make the forms manifested from one's thoughts into idols and worship them as deities is called *pūjā*.

purānas (T)   Hindu scriptures; mythologies; legends; epics. The stories of each religion can be described as *purānas*. One religion calls it the Bible, another calls it the Qur'an. Some stories were sent down as commandments from God, others were created through man's intelligence and senses, while still others were created by poets, usually as songs of praise depicting stories.

qalb (A)   The heart within the heart of man; the inner heart. Bawa explains that there are two states for the *qalb* and four chambers. The four chambers are earth, fire, air, and water—representing Hinduism, Fire Worship, Christianity, and Islam. Inside these four chambers there is a flower, the flower of the *qalb* which is the divine qualities of God. This is the flower of grace [*Rahmat*]. It is called the *qalb*. In this *qalb* only His fragrance exists.

The other four chambers are black. They are really the dog [*kalb*], the black dog which is the world and thoughts of the world and of the five elements. But Allah's truth and His fragrance is that flower of the heart. That is the kingdom of Allah's church or mosque. There are some who worship in the darkness and some who worship in the light. Those who worship within that flower are worshiping in the light. One section is light and the other four sections are the night.

Qur'ān (A)   The words of God that were revealed to His messenger, Prophet Muhammad (*Sal.*). Those words that came from His power are called the Qur'an. The Qur'an is the explanation of Allah's qualities, actions, and duties; of *'ālam* [the universe] and *arwāh* [the world of the souls]; of His creations; and of the prophets who came before and the prophets who came after. The Qur'an reveals these explanations to the people, the prophets, the saints, the angels, the heavenly beings, the *qutbs*, the jinns, the fairies, and all created beings in order to demonstrate and explain His qualities and actions.

This Qur'an also exists within the heart of man. The qualities which are God's state of truth, His duties, and His actions, together form the Qur'an. This can be seen on the outside and on the inside. What is seen on the outside are the commandments, but what is seen on the inside is the explanation of God's qualities and actions, His beauty, plenitude, and completeness. Understanding what is seen outside is merely learning from example. If it is understood within, it will be called the essence of Allah [*Zāt*]. If one goes on studying and understanding from the outside that is *sharī'at*, while inside it is *haqīqat* or *ma'rifat*. In this way, climbing step by step by step, and understanding within, we must climb one quality to understand the next quality and to transcend wisdom. We must climb holding onto God's duties. This is the study on the inside. If we understand within, this is the inner Qur'an. If we recite the Qur'an from within, we will see Allah as the One, the one truth, the only One worthy of worship, and we will see only one family. But if we recite the Qur'an and try to understand it on the outside, we will see many meanings, many divisions, many states, and many differences. This is why Muhammad, the Messenger of Allah (*Sal.*), has said, "Go even unto China to learn *'Ilm* [divine knowledge]." What does this mean? One meaning is that we must learn wisdom from within.

Rahmat (A) God's grace; His forgiveness and compassion; His benevolence; His wealth. To all creations, He is the wealth of life [*hayāt*] and the wealth of *Īmān* [absolute faith, certitude, and determination]. All the good things that we receive from God are called His *Rahmat*. That is the wealth of God's plenitude. Everything that is within God is *Rahmat*, and if He were to give that grace, that would be an undiminishing, limitless wealth. Everything that has been discarded from Him is worldly wealth and treasures. Those treasures can perish and be destroyed and are subject to change. The word *rahmat* can also be used for those worldly treasures that change with the seasons. But the *Rahmat* of Allah will never change for all time. That is why it is the greatest, most valuable treasure to anyone who receives it.

rak'at (A) A bow followed by two prostrations in the five times prayer of Islam.

rasool (A) Apostle or messenger; one who has wisdom, faith in God, and good qualities; one who behaves with respect and dignity toward his fellow men. A *rasool* is one who has completely accepted only God and has rejected everything else; one who has accepted God's divine words, His qualities and actions, and puts them into practice. Those who from time immemorial have given the divine laws of God to the people and who have such a connection with God are called a prophet [*nabī*] or *rasool*. The name *rasool* has been given even to the angels. *Rasool* is often used as a name for Prophet Muhammad (*Sal.*).

Rūh (A) The soul; the light ray of God; the light of God's wisdom.

Bawa explains *Rūh* to also mean life or *hayāt*. Out of the six kinds of lives, it is the light-life, the ray of the light of *Noor* which does not die. It does not disappear; it is the truth. It does not die; it exists forever. That soul has obtained the wealth of *mubārakāt* [the unperishable treasure of all three worlds]. It is Allah's grace [*Rahmat*]. It is called light-life. The other five lives appear and disappear. They are called earth-life, fire-life, water-life, air-life, and ether-life. The *Rūh* is the light-life.

rūhānī (A) The spirit of the elements. There are six kinds of lives within man. One is human life which is the light-life. That is the soul [*Rūh*]. Associated with this are the lives of earth, fire, water, air, and ether. These constitute the *rūhānī*.

When all the four hundred trillion, ten thousand intentions and thoughts take form, they are called *rūhānīs*. All the things to which the mind roams in its thoughts are called *rūhānīs*. Even after a person dies, his desires being him back. It is those desires, those *rūhānīs*, that bring him back to be born again.

saboor (A) Inner patience; to go within patience, to practice it, to think and reflect within it.

Saboor is that patience deep within patience which comforts, soothes, and alleviates mental suffering. The next stage is *shukoor*, normally called contentment. *Shukoor* is deep within *saboor*, pacifying and comforting. Even deeper within *shukoor*, still more soothing and comforting, is *tawakkal-Allāh* [absolute trust in Allah]. And deep within *tawakkal-Allāh*, giving comfort and contentment, is *Alhamdulillāh*—surrendering all responsibility to Him. "There is nothing left in my hands." Total surrender. "I have given up everything, I am helpless, I am undone."

Saboor, *shukoor*, *tawakkal-Allāh*, *Alhamdulillāh*—these are the treasures of *Īmān* [absolute faith, certitude, and determination]. The wealth of patience is the preface to *Īmān* and is the exalted wisdom [*Gnānam*] in the life of a true man [*Insān*]. To possess these four and to act by them are the four most important duties [*fardhs*] for *Īmān-Islām*. These four are the preface to *Īmān*.

Yā Saboor—one of the 99 names of Allah. God, who is in a state of limitless patience, forgives the faults of His created beings and continues to protect them.

saddu (T)   Life or essence.

sakti (T)   A force or energy. In Tamil, the word *sakti* refers to *siva-sakti*. *Sakti* is the consort of *Siva* [both are Hindu deities]. In Arabic it is *Ādam* and *Hawwā'*, and in Christianity it is Adam and Eve. They are the one original father and mother, but they are given various names and meanings in the different religions and languages.

(Sal.) (A)   Abbreviations for *Sallallāhu 'alaihi wa sallam*.

salaam (A)   The peace of God. Greetings! There are many meanings to the word *salaam*. When we say *salaam*, it means 'in God's name' or 'in the presence of God'. In the presence of God, both of us become one without any division; both of us are in a state of unity, a state of peace.

salawāt (A)   Plural of *salat*, prayer; usually used for the supplication asking God to bless the prophets and mankind. See also: *Sallallāhu 'alaihi wa sallam*.

Sallallāhu 'alaihi wa salaam (A)   God bless him and grant him salvation. A supplication traditionally spoken after mentioning the name of Prophet Muhammad *(Sal.)*. It is frequently abbreviated as *(Sal.)*.

All beings created by God have been granted peace or have attained peace because of the *Rasool*, Prophet Muhammad *(Sal.)*. Saying "*Sallallāhu 'alaihi wa salaam*" therefore means: "In the same way that you gave peace to us, may all the people who follow the *Rasool* be blessed with eternal and undiminishing peace." This supplication is also referred to as the *salawāt*.

shaddah (A)   An Arabic diacritical mark which, when placed over a letter, indicates that the letter is doubled.

shari (T)   Right. Bawa uses this Tamil word to give meaning to the similar sounding Arabic word *sharī'at*.

sharī'at, tarīqat, haqīqat, and *ma'rifat* (A)   The four steps of spiritual ascendance:

sharī'at—the realization of good and evil and conducting one's life according to the good.

tarīqat—unswerving and complete acceptance of the good and carrying out of every action accordingly.

haqīqat—the realization of Divinity and the beginning of communication with God.

ma'rifat—the state of merging with God.

sharr (A)   That which is wrong, bad or evil; as opposed to *khair* [right].

shukoor (A)   Contentment; the state within *saboor* [inner patience]; that which is kept within the treasure chest of patience.

Yā Shakoor—one of the 99 beautiful names of Allah. To do *shukoor* with the help of the One who is *Shakoor* is true *shukoor*. See also: *saboor*.

sifāt (A)   The manifestation of creation; attributes; all that has come into appearance as form; that which arose from the word "*Kun!* [Be!]"

sūfīyat (A)   The fifth level of spiritual ascendance. The state of one who has transcended the four religions and has merged with God.

In the station of *sūfīyat*, one speaks without talking, sees without looking, hears without listening, relishes fragrances without smelling, and learns without studying. That learning cannot be known, and that understanding cannot be understood. These and many other such states come with acquiring the qualities of God and losing oneself within those qualities. Although one still exists within the body, he has built within himself the palace of Divine Luminous Wisdom. One who has perfected this state is a *sūfī*.

The word *sūfī* is used loosely and many meanings are attributed to it. But a true *sūfī* is one who has beaten the world and chased it away, one who has beaten the mind and chased it away, one who has beaten his faults away from himself, one who has understood and realized himself, one who has come to know his Lord, one who has rejected everything else and lost himself within God. Such excellence is the state of *sūfīyat*. He has extricated himself from the ten sins and has lost himself within the two—the *Noor* and God. He has disappeared within the *Noor* and lost himself within God. That is *sūfīyat*.

sukoon (A)   A circle 'o'; an Arabic diacritical mark which indicates a vowelless consonant.

sūrat, sūrah (A)   A chapter of the Qur'an. Spelled in Arabic with a different 's' it means form, shape, pictorial representation, illustration, figure, or statue.

Sūratul-Baqarah (A) The second chapter of the Qur'an; 'The Chapter of the Heifer'.

Sūratul-Fātihah (A) The opening chapter of the Qur'an, also called the *Alhamdu Sūrah*; the inner form of man; the clarity of understanding the four elements of the body (earth, fire, water, air); and the realization of the self and of Allah within. The *Sūratul-Fātihah* must be recited at the beginning of every prayer. Within man is the *Sūratul-Fātihah*, and within the *Sūratul-Fātihah* is the inner form of man. If we split open that form, we can see within it Allah's words, His qualities, His actions, His 3,000 divine attributes, and His 99 *wilāyats*, or powers. It is also called the *Sūratul-Insān*, or the inner form of man.

The *Sūratul-Fātihah* must be split open with wisdom to see all these within. It must be split open by the ocean of divine knowledge [*Bahrul-'Ilm*]. Opening his heart [*qalb*], opening his form [*sūrat*] and looking within, having his own form looking at his own form—that is the *Sūratul-Fātihah*. What is recited on the outside is the *Alhamdu Sūrah*. The two meanings differ in this manner: the outer one is a meaning on the level of *sharī'at* [the first level of spiritual ascendance]; the inner meaning relates to the essence of *Zāt*. *Fātihah* means literally to open out. It is opening the heart [*qalb*] and looking within.

Sūratul-Insān (A) The inner form of man. The inner form of man [*Sūratul-Insān*] is the Qur'an and is formed out of the 28 letters. This form [*sūrat*] is the *Ummul-Qur'ān*. This form is the Qur'an in which the revelations of Allah are revealed. The sounds in the Qur'an which resonate through wisdom, the Messenger of Allah, Prophet Muhammad (*Sal.*), the angels and heavenly beings—all are made to exist in this body as secrets. They can be seen in these letters.

One has to recite that Qur'an, analyze and understand the meaning of each letter, make the sounds resonate through wisdom, speak with them, merge with them, and go within the Qur'an which is Allah's revelations.

Through this Qur'an man can understand the chapters [*sūrats*] and commands of Allah, the 6,666 verses [*āyats*], the traditional stories [*hadīsz*], this world [*dunyā*], the prophets who came before and the prophets who came after, the angels and the heavenly beings, the 18,000 universes and their meanings, the explanations of true man [*Insān*], the explanations of the commands of Allah, the explanations of hell and heaven, the soul [rūh] and the elemental spirits [rūhānīs], jinns and fairies, idols and satan. To understand all these, to eliminate those which must be eliminated, to make the truth of Allah resonate, to dispel the darkness and take on the qualities of Allah, and to merge within Him on the path of worship—that is the *Ummul-Qur'ān* within the heart of a true man [*Insān*], giving explanations and clarity. See also: *Sūratul Fātihah*.

Sūratul Qur'ān (A)   The inner form of the Qur'an; the body made of the 28 Arabic letters. Man's *sūrat* [form] has been formed by the Qur'an; that is the *Sūratul Qur'ān*. See also: *Tiru Qur'ān*.

Sūratur-Rahmān (A)   A chapter of the Qur'an.

Sūratu Yā Sīn (A)   A chapter of the Qur'an often referred to as the heart of the Qur'an.

tantra (T)   A trick; a cunning trick performed with a selfish motive of self-praise or self-gain.

taripadu (T)   To make firm. Bawa often uses this Tamil word to give meaning to the similar sounding Arabic word *tarīqat* [the second step of spiritual ascendance].

tarīqat (A)   The second step of spiritual ascendance; unswerving and complete acceptance of good and carrying out every action accordingly. See also: *sharī'at*.

tawakkal-Allāh or *tawakkul* (A)   Absolute trust and surrender; handing over to God the entire responsibility for everything. Same as *Allāhu Wakeel*—You are my Trustee, my Lawyer, my Guardian.

Yā Wakeel, one of the 99 beautiful names of Allah.

they or *sza'* (A)   An Arabic letter (ث).

toluhai (T)   Worship; the performance of true prayer or *'ibādat* where one remembers only God to the exclusion of everything else.

vanakkum (T)   Prayer. There are 1,000 million kinds of prayer.

waqt (A)   Time of prayer. In the religion of Islam there are five specified *waqts*, or times of prayer, each day.

Truly, there is only one *waqt*. That is the prayer that never ends, where one is in direct communication with God and one is merged in God.

wilāyat (A)   God's power; that which has been revealed and manifested through God's actions; the miraculous names and actions of God; the power of His attributes through which all creations came into existence.

Zaboor, Jabrāt, Injeel, and Furqān (A)   The four religions or the four steps of spiritual ascendance. The inner form of man [Sūratul-Insān] is made up of the four religions. The four religions constitute his body. The first is the religion in which he appeared, the creation of his form, the religion in which forms are created. That is Zaboor, Hinduism. In the body, this relates to the area below the waist. Second is Jabrāt, Fire Worship. This relates to hunger, disease, and old age. This is the religion of the stomach. Third is Injeel, Christianity. This is the area of the heart. This heart is filled with thoughts, emotions, spirits, vapors, many tens of millions of forms, the five elements, mind and desire, and four hundred trillion, ten thousand spiritual worships. Fourth is Furqān, the religion sent down to Moses and Muhammad (Sal.). This corresponds to the head. It is made up of the seven causes (two eyes, two ears, two nostrils, and one mouth), and it will give explanations through these.

To study these four religions as four steps and to understand them, to study the differences and understand the difference between good and evil, that is the head. The head is the leader or chief for all four religions. If there is no head, the form cannot be identified; there are no identifying marks. It is the head that sees with the identifying signs. To see with the eyes; to hear with the ears; to smell through the nostrils; to speak or taste with the mouth; to give information and explain through wisdom; to transmit explanations to the qalb or heart; to realize and understand the difference between good and evil; to take whatever is good and show it and transmit the meaning to the heart—that is Furqān. The head of every man is called Furqān.

There are the Sūratul-Insān and the Sūratul-Fātihah. It is the sūrat [body-form] that is man, or Insān. The wisdom that is capable of inspecting and analyzing this body is within him. Allah has given him the essence [Zāt] to know and understand the manifestations of creation [sifāts]. Knowing this, to take up what is good and discard what is evil is Furqān. These four religions form the body of man, and the religion of Furqān helps man to understand these. For divine knowledge ['Ilm] these are four steps, but for the intellect they exist as four religions. And *Furqān* is that which makes this explanation complete.

Lit.: *Zaboor*—the religion given to David, the psalms of David; *Jabrāt* (*Jabrūt*)—a stage in sufi terminology denoting the sphere of knowledge or station where one discards personal power and becomes assimilated into the power of God. *Injeel*—the Gospels. *Furqān*—the criterion of right and wrong; the Qur'an; also the revelations given to Moses.

Zāt (A)   The essence of God; His treasury; His wealth of purity; His grace.

Zikr (A)   The *wilāyats* [powers] of Allah and His grace have been praised in so many ways. The *Zikr* is a common name given to those words of praise. Out of those *Zikrs*, the most exalted *Zikr* is to say, "*Lā ilāha ill Allāhu* [Other than You there is no God. Only You are Allah]." That is the most exalted *Zikr*. All the others relate to His *wilāyats*, or His actions, but this *Zikr* points to Him and to Him alone.

INDEX

Abdullah: 21. *See also* Muhammad (*Sal.*), parents of

Adam, 3, 4

Amina: 21. *See also* Muhammad (*Sal.*), parents of

Abu Jahil, 20, 21

Abu Talib, 21-23

'Ali, 22

Abu Bakr, 22

Christianity (*Injeel*): 5, 10; mentioned 19; 27-29, 36-40. *See also* haqīqat

Creation, 18

Destruction, 7, 13

Diacritical marks, 40-42

Fire worship (*Jabrāt, Hanal*): 5, 10; mentioned 19; 27-29; 36-40. *See also* tarīqat.

Gabriel, 22

Gnānam, eye of: 3,4. *See also* Kursī, Noor

God: point of, 2; awareness of, 3; merging with, 10, 11, 39; qualities of, 19; as a mirror, 42

Habib, King, 21-23

Haqīqat: 27-29; 36-40; mentioned 19; *See also* Christianity

Hinduism (*Zaboor*): 5, 9; mentioned 19; 27-29; 36-40. *See also* sharī'at

Īmān: 10, 11; 36; prerequisites of, 37, 38

Īmān-Islām, 37

Insān Kāmil, 14, 30

Islam (*Furqān*): 5, 11; mentioned 19; 27-29; 36-40. *See also* ma'rifat

Khadījah: 21, 22. *See also* Muhammad (*Sal.*), wife of

Ka'bah, 24

Kursī: 3. *See also* Gnānam, Noor

Mecca, 21

Mind: how to deal with, 38

Miracles, 6

Ma'rifat: 27-29; 36-40; mentioned 19. *See also* Islam

Muhammad, Prophet (*Sal.*): attempts to kill, 20; parents of, 21; wife of, 21; proof of prophethood, 23. *See also* Abdullah; Amina; Khadījah

Noor: 3, 4; *See also* Gnānam, Kursī

Prayer: 8, 9, 12-14, 16, 18, 19, 30, 35, 36, 42-44

Qur'an, 23, 41

Religions: development of, 4; divisions within, 4, 5; stages of life corresponding to, 27-28

Sharī'at: 27-29, 36-40; mentioned 19. See also Hinduism

Seven causal signs, 40-41

Sūfīyat, 15, 29, 42

Tarīqat: 27-29; 36-40; mentioned 19; See also fire worship

'Usman, 22

'Umar, 22

Unity, 34, 35

World: deception of, 31

Worship: of forms, 6; places of, 5; how to, 29. See also fire worship

Other books by His Holiness M. R. Bawa Muhaiyaddeen

Truth & Light

Songs of God's Grace

*The Divine Luminous Wisdom
that Dispels the Darkness*

*The Guidebook
to the True Secret of the Heart
(Volume One and Volume Two)*

God, His Prophets and His Children

*Asma'ul-Husna:
The 99 Beautiful Names of Allah*

*The Truth and Unity of Man
Letters in Response to a Crisis*

The Wisdom of Man

The central branch of the Bawa Muhaiyaddeen Fellowship is located in Philadelphia and serves as Bawa's residence while he is in the United States. The Fellowship also serves as a meeting house and as a reservoir of people and materials for all who are interested in the teachings of Bawa Muhaiyaddeen. For information write or call:

The Bawa Muhaiyaddeen Fellowship
5820 Overbrook Avenue
Philadelphia, Pennsylvania 19131

Telephone: (215) 879-8631